Ramsgate to Ranish,
a walk through Britain

Valerie Hamilton

Published by New Generation Publishing in 2023

Copyright © Valerie Hamilton 2023
Illustrations by Mary Hamilton, facebook @ M. H. art

First Edition

ISBN: 978-1-80369-899-1

www.newgeneration-publishing.com

New Generation Publishing

Preface

This is an account of a walk through Britain which was the fulfilment of a nearly life-time dream. I set out to revisit the places I had lived and to see the length of the land. In doing so I discovered so much I did not know about the country and met many lovely people. The walk was so much more than I expected. At times it pushed me out of my comfort zone and almost broke me but at other times it was almost relaxing and therapeutic.

Talking to passers by I realised there are many people with unfulfilled dreams, some expressed a desire to undertake a walk or adventure. I hope this book inspires someone to take the step and 'go for it', to realise their dream. At least I hope it encourages people to get out there and go for walks and discover the plethora of footpaths in Britain and the great countryside, sometimes peace and quiet where you least expect it.

Ramsgate to Ranish

WHW - West Highland Way
GGW - Great Glen Way
.... route walked
- - - - bus or train
ferry

Finish
Ranish
Ullapool
Inverness
Fort Augustus
Fort William
Tyndrum
Edinburgh
Glasgow
Kirk Yetholm
Pennine Way
Edale
Wirral
Frodsham
Wrexham
King's Lynn
Necton
Hay on Wye
Pirton
Brecon
Cheltenham
Hitchin
Lydbrook
London
Start
Maidstone
Ramsgate

Chapter 1; beginnings

I had fallen off my map. I was looking out on 'unmapped' land or rather land not on any of the maps I was carrying. It made me think of the helicopter pilots in Roald Dahl's 'Big Friendly Giant' when they fall off the last page of their world atlas and are on the blank pages found at the back of the book. Hopefully I was walking the right way and if I followed the edge of the field would fall back on to the relevant map I was carrying.

It was the middle of the third week of my long walk through Britain and I was in central England heading towards Dunstable Downs. It wasn't so very far from where I grew up but far enough to be beyond the distance we walked on day walks from the village. The stubble field stretched far ahead bordered by a dull winter hedge, to my left was the line of the Chiltern hills and overhead a pale winter sun seeped through the clouds. I adjusted my rucksack on my back and continued walking.

The seed of the idea for the walk had been growing in my head for years, ever since as a young adult I had been given the book 'Journey through Britain' by John Hillaby. It is his account of his walk from Land's End to John O'Groats in the mid-1960's. I had travelled little at that time, much of Britain was unknown territory. It made me realise it was possible to walk the length of Britain, I resolved to do so on retirement. I had grown up to love walking but it wasn't until my children were older that I began long distance back-packing. In the past fifteen years I had undertaken numerous back-packing trips in mid-Wales and northern Scotland. Initially trips were with three of my children but increasingly they were solo walks. The routes were always through wild upland areas and I had never back-packed in England.

A walk entails a route. Interestingly John Hillaby describes long distance walkers as a dying breed in the 1960's, now it is more popular than ever. It is possible to look on the internet and access a route from Land's End to John O'Groats (LEJOG) or to 'steal' someone else's route from reading their account of their own walk. In 1987 I had cycled with a friend from John O'Groats to Land's End (JOGLE) in two weeks. We had planned our own itinerary, staying in friend's houses and youth hostels then taken torn out pages of a road atlas to follow. It hadn't been a 'normal' JOGLE route, we had detoured to friends, family and a wedding.

Rather than following a LEJOG route, I wanted to create my own route, a route with a meaning, a personal pilgrimage through Britain. At the end of 2017 we had moved as a family to the Isle of Lewis, the largest island making up the Outer Hebrides off the North West coast of Scotland. Thinking about the various places I had lived in England I decided to revisit them, the walk would be through my past to the present. Additionally I could visit friends which would hopefully mean places to stay, otherwise there was my trusty tent.

Maps strewed the floor as I planned a way through Britain, searching for footpaths to link up the places I wanted to pass through. The internet revealed a wealth of long-distance footpaths which I could dip in and out of across the land. I had no connection to Cornwall but I had lived in Kent so that meant the Kent coast would be the ideal starting point. I plumped for Ramsgate, partly because some friends live nearby and also because Ramsgate to Ranish (my village on the Isle of Lewis) has a good ring to it. I planned to walk north to the edge of London, visit former homes there, then head out to Hertfordshire where I grew up. A detour to Norfolk before heading west to Gloucestershire. A meander through the Welsh borders to relatives on the Wirral then a hop across to Sheffield to stay with friends. The Pennine Way is a long-distance path I had always wanted to walk, that would take me into Scotland. A wiggle east to Edinburgh and Fife and then a simple north west route to the ferry at Ullapool and so home. All sounded quite easy! A rough tally of the miles came to 1200. I calculated three months would be an adequate time-scale for the walk, I could be flexible though, not having any deadlines to get back for.

Having planned the route and tentatively contacted friends to ask about visiting them (this was still during the covid-19 pandemic), I then had the great idea of visiting parkruns too. Parkruns are free, weekly, timed 5 kilometre runs or walks organised in many parts of the country and abroad. I could visit a parkrun each week to add another dimension to my trip and meet local people. Parkruns are sparse though in some parts of the country, notably the Cotswolds and Shropshire but amazingly with only a little tweaking of the route and juggling with days I found I could go to one every Saturday until the Pennine Way. There were also a couple in Scotland on my way through.

The question was then, when to walk? Summer was out of the question as we are developing a market garden and so summers are busy producing and selling vegetables. Added to that I didn't want to walk in the excessively hot summers which England seems to experience and summers in Scotland mean midges, not much fun when camping. Autumn would involve walking into increasingly shorter days and arriving in Scotland in the winter. I decided to leave then in January and walk in to the lengthening days of spring.

The plan had been to wait until I was turning sixty but the covid-19 epidemic with the resultant lockdowns and travel restrictions gave the impetus to walk a year earlier. I wanted to see a post covid Britain and was fearful of further travel restrictions with the emergence of the omicron variant of covid.

By 2022 travel was allowed, my family told me to go (they obviously wanted to get rid of me) so I packed my rucksack. On 12th January 2022 I caught the bus to Stornoway, then the ferry to mainland Scotland for the start of my journey south to begin my long walk back home.

Chapter 2

Through Kent; mud & motorways

15th-21st January

It was 7am when I slipped out of the air bnb in the dark, to allow plenty of time to reach my first parkrun at Pegwell Bay starting at 9am. All was quiet in the streets of Ramsgate, no one was around, just the birds beginning to sing. It was good to now be on my way, my long walk had begun. Leaving town, it became light with the promise of good weather. It was only 7.30am, back home it would not become this light until 9am, I had gained over an hour's daylight simply by being in the south of England.

It had taken me over two days to arrive in Ramsgate; leaving on an afternoon ferry and spending the first night in Inverness, followed by a night in Edinburgh before reaching Ramsgate. It was useful to have a slow journey as I had not been to a town larger than Stornoway for over a year and so made use of my time in Inverness to shop for last minute items for the walk. That included a pair of walking trousers which came with loads of pockets, very useful when walking (though only by buying the men's version, the lady's version for some reason had no cargo pocket and few other pockets, are women supposed to walk with handbags?) I binned the pair of trousers I had travelled in which felt wrong, but they were old and ragged.

I had managed to buy cheap train tickets so travelled all the way from Inverness to London by train. I was relieved that I arrived at King's Cross station and only had to walk to St Pancras for the final train and not tackle the tube. Travelling south from Inverness, first Scotland and then England passed by the train window so quickly. How many weeks would it take me to walk back that way? Something of the enormity of the walk struck me. I had travelled the trainline to Edinburgh forty years ago to and from St Andrew's university and noticed the changes in the land. Vast wind turbines interrupting the horizons and so many new houses and warehouse developments on the edge of towns and villages as we got further south. It felt like Britain was becoming one vast building site.

Arriving in a warm and sunny Ramsgate, fifty hours after leaving home, I walked down to the sea front. It felt like summer, not early January, it was so warm! I sat by the harbour minus hat and coat, looking at the boats and the passing people. My impression of Ramsgate was somewhere struggling and run down, there were many empty shops in the town centre and rubbish littering the streets, not helped by the fact that the shops were in deep shade. Piles of donated goods sat outside the 'Happy Horse Sanctuary' charity shop. It appeared to be closed down so I wasn't sure why the goods weren't taken to another of the many charity shops in town. I was amazed at the number of 'vape' shops (I had never seen one before), as well as 'pound' shops and pawnshops. There was a cheery atmosphere down by the promenade though with 'hippie' folk sitting outside a pub and some families walking on the beach and along the sea wall. Smartly dressed grammar school children appeared on their way home. The beach was well trodden, orange sand stretching as far as the eye could see, a line of wind turbines heading out to sea from nearby Margate. France was a hazy dark shadow on the horizon, emphasising how far south I was in Britain. A friendly couple on the beach kindly took a photo of myself in front of the Royal pavilion, proof that I had started there. Ramsgate is one of the coastal towns of the Isle of Thanet along with Margate, Broadstairs and Cliftonville. My parents had honeymooned somewhere here in December 1959 so by beginning here I was walking in their past too.

A cliff path leads out of the town passing the last few houses on the right and a new-build site on the left, disturbingly close to the crumbling cliff edge. How long will the house be there? The cliffs are rather collapsing and unpronounced all the way to Cliffs End where I found a replica Viking's ship. From a distance I took it to be part of a children's play park but no it is a full-size replica Viking ship. Built in Denmark and sailed over the channel by fifty-three Danish men in 1949 then left on this side. I wondered if the Kent people had bought it off the Danes or not or had they just not wanted to sail it back again? I presume they returned to their country another way or was this the last invasion of Britain? The body of the ship was covered with a tarpaulin to protect it from the weather over the winter which made it look rather forlorn.

Pegwell Bay did not take as long to reach as I had expected, I arrived there an hour early for parkrun. I stood on the beach and watched a red sun rise out of the sea and chatted to the men who run the café there. It was a good introduction to being questioned about my walk and people's responses to it, as at parkrun I became a bit of a celebrity because of it! The other runners and volunteers were a friendly bunch. Pegwell Bay is a very nice parkrun, two flat laps along good tracks past the shore and through woodland. I found it amusing at the start as you run towards bollards with volunteers standing against them shouting "bollard" to prevent accidents! I think that standing there facing sixty plus runners coming towards you would be quite scary and wondered how many volunteers had been run into! My wings flew me round the course, narrowly missing first female place in 23:46, my second quickest parkrun time ever and only the second time I have achieved sub 24 minutes! The benefits of a flat course and no wind, plus perhaps lazy days travelling.

It was a good morale boost as I changed into walking clothes and boots, shouldering my pack for my first day's walk. It was not too far as I was going to stay with my friends near Ash some six miles away. I was glad of a short first day as it always takes time to adjust to carrying 13kg or so on your back. With the three miles already walked to parkrun I would still cover nine miles in a day plus the three-mile run. My plan was to follow the England Coast path and then cross over the river Stour on a small footbridge I had spotted on my map. This would get me on the correct side of the river to follow the Stour Valley Way past Richborough castle and then pick up footpaths to Upper Goldstone farm where Jacqueline and Andrew live.

The coastal path through the nature reserve was lovely, numerous birds were taking advantage of a large lagoon and long-horn cattle grazed the rough grass. A strange squeaking noise was being made by some of the birds, it rather sounded like lots of squeaky toys. A bird watcher explained it was the noise of the numerous lapwing tumbling above the water. After a mile there was a notice; "due to commercial works on the coast there is an alternative route". I followed this alternative route which leads to the A256, it shortly became a dual-carriageway. There is a wide cycle/footpath beside it but in no stretch of the imagination is it a *coast* path. My map was old and still showed the road as an A road and not a dual-carriageway. Being hopeless with technology I rely on ordnance survey maps and for my walk had cut out the relevant sections of maps to save on weight. I had also bought a lot of my maps second-hand so some dated back to 1985 and even newer maps may not have been updated that recently. I decided to retrace my steps to see if it was possible to walk along the coast.

After the notice announcing the alternative route the path deteriorated, leading through a broken fence and undergrowth to the shore at an old jetty. Seals lazed on a sandbank and a little egret pottered about. The path then just fizzled out at a junkyard. A harmless, friendly tramp emerged from the bushes and informed me that you couldn't go beyond the quay on the river. He added that it was a good place to camp, a slightly dubious claim as he then said that his tent had been set on fire there!

I had no option but to return to the main road and regretted not researching this section of the walk better beforehand, I had naively looked at the map and presumed I could follow the coast. I was accustomed to emptier lands and the 'right to roam' law in Scotland. For over one and half miles the England coast path follows a busy dual-carriageway through uninspiring countryside. Not surprisingly no one else was walking along it though there were lots of friendly cyclists. I still wanted to cross the little bridge over the River Stour marked on my map. It turned out to be accessed via a recycling centre on the other side of the dual-carriageway. There was no crossing point over the road and a metal crash barrier down the middle. Dodging quickly through a gap in the traffic I made it over the road in one piece and strode purposely down the drive of the recycling centre towards the bridge which I noticed was the other side of a spiky fence.

"Where are you going?" challenged the recycling man.

"To the bridge" I replied.

"You can't go across it" he retorted.

I had already worked out how to bypass the spikes and get on to the bridge safely.

"It isn't allowed" he stated, looking at a colleague who had joined him for support.

I suggested that they wouldn't see me but they insisted I might injure myself. I tried to point out that walking beside the busy road was very injurious but to no avail. I had no choice but to recross the dual-carriageway and re-join the 'coast' path.

The coast path route leads all the way into Sandwich past the former Pfizzer factory which is now The Discovery Centre, a vast semi-derelict science park for medical research. Eventually the River Stour is crossed on an old stone bridge at Sandwich, smart yachts are tied up to the quay. Sandwich is a lovely historic town of narrow streets and flint-stone faced houses. Many of the houses front right on the road or the pavement and have attractive brass handles and door-knockers on their stout wooden doors. I resisted the temptation of knocking on them as I walked past. Later when I mentioned this to my friends, Andrew said he had thought a photographic book of all the doors entitled 'Knobs and knockers of Sandwich' would sell well!

It was lunchtime when I reached Richborough castle, an old Roman fort and amphitheatre. It was closed so I climbed over the fence to sit on a bench in the sun, there was no one to stop me. An early butterfly fluttered around. From there it was a short walk over fields and through orchards to my friends where I planned to spend two nights. And thus ended the first day's walk.

I set out early on the Monday morning after a restful Sunday with my friends. It was cold and frosty, the sun just rising and no wind. The forecast for the next few days was good. I had a sixteen-mile day planned to get me beyond Canterbury and on to the North Downs Way. To reach Canterbury I followed the Stour Valley walk along quiet roads and through orchards and fields. Rotting apples lay on the ground and some apples still hung from the trees. Flocks of red-wing chattered in the orchards mixed at times with the screeching of parakeets who were released in London some time back and have now spread to surrounding counties. I saw my first snowdrops and daffodils in front gardens. Glum faced drivers passed on the narrow winding roads, forcing me to squeeze against the hedges to enable them to pass. None acknowledged my presence, the lone back-packer was invisible to them.

As the frost thawed I discovered how tacky Kent mud is, something that would plague me for the next few days. It sticks to your boots gradually building up so that they become twice their size until chunks of mud drop off or you reach grass where you can attempt to clean it off only to gain more in the next muddy field. The Ash levels are incredibly flat, nowhere being more than five metres above sea level. The river Stour in Saxon times was the old shore line helping to create the Isle of Thanet which as I had discovered was still like an island nowadays when it came to leaving it.

Reaching the river near Upstreet I stopped. My walking system is to set off early and have a rest after a couple of hours and something to eat, then to stop again in a couple more hours for lunch. I prefer to walk further in the mornings and take afternoons slower when I am tired, also in January the afternoons were very short. The day was warm, I removed my hat and jacket then headed off through Stodmarsh nature reserve. The reeds shone golden in the sun but the paths were thick mud and it was a struggle to not slide over, my walking poles were useful. Birds were singing though they all seemed to be hidden in the reeds. Meeting the road I climbed the first hill of my walk, to 26metres above sea level! It seemed quite an effort after the flat land and I hoped all hills wouldn't feel that hard! I entered lovely chestnut coppiced woodland, something I encountered a lot in Kent, the ground a carpet of dull, gold coloured three fingered leaves. Woodpeckers were busy drumming on the trees and jays squawked.

In the old village of Fordwich I stopped for lunch in the churchyard and chatted to a cyclist from nearby Canterbury. On hearing about my walk the conversation focused on origins and where people feel they belong; he had grown up in Aberdeen, had ancestors from the Orkneys but had lived in Kent for many years so questioned where he belonged. He asked me where I would say 'home' was. I replied that having moved around I looked on where I lived at the moment as home but my family home as the village I grew up in. Perhaps people in Scotland have the right approach as where you live is referred to as where you *stay* and where you or your family originate from as where you are *from*. I spoke of the hopelessness I felt there was in Ramsgate and he commented that the people there feel neglected by the government and threatened with an influx of asylum seekers. It was an interesting thought-provoking chat.

Approaching the city of Canterbury I lost the route in rough woodland and came across a make-shift wooden enclosure with tents inside, presumably where people are living. Was this through choice of lifestyle or through a lack of housing? Hopefully the former reason but probably the second. Canterbury is a city of two faces; the beautiful touristy side with the cathedral and old town with quaint shops and the rather poor housing estates further out. I felt there was a big divide. Walking past the tourists and the cathedral in my muddy boots and my large pack I felt rather out of place, everyone was respectfully dressed. Old council housing estates give access to the North Downs Way which initially runs below an embankment of the A2. The stench of rubbish thrown down into the trees from a layby on the road above was overpowering. The rest of the day was through chestnut woods and orchards, including an ancient apple orchard on no man's land between two parishes. There are also large commercial farms with extensive areas of static caravans for the migrant workers. In post Brexit Britain it was surprising that there were still workers from further east in Europe.

I camped at dusk in a strip of woodland beside the track and watched the sun set as an orange ball and the full moon rise. It felt strange to be camped by a track where someone might pass as I was used to camping in lonely mountain valleys. It was a bright night, the trees creating shadows on my tent, there was no need for a torch. I heated up some water on my gas stove and made a 'cuppa soup'. I drank it while some instant noodles cooked and added some cheese to them. This was to be my staple dinners on my walk with the variation of couscous or quick pasta and tinned fish. In the evening I lay in my sleeping bag nibbling biscuits and chocolate looking out at the moonlit land. I left the door of the outer tent wide open so I could look out at the moon during the night. There wasn't any wind and it was cosy with the inner tent zipped up, listening to foxes and owls. In the background was the noise of traffic and the occasional train, such noises only ceasing in the small hours.

In the morning, mist covered the valley, the hedges and trees rising out of the mist in a chequered pattern. I studied the days route and how much food I had and realised I could be on short rations for the day. Often I carry five days supply of food, if not going through any places, but in England I knew most days I would be passing a shop which meant my pack could be lighter. However I wasn't sure if the next couple of villages had shops and so until late in the day all I had left was half a banana, one bread roll, some chocolate and a handful of dates. I certainly wouldn't starve but would have felt happier with more supplies.

I walked through the delightful sounding village of Old Wives Lees, or OWLS for short, a friendly place where everyone said hello and car drivers waved. There was a protest notice about the proposed nearby solar farm which will cover the equivalent of eighty-six football pitches. Similar notices about proposed developments cropped up daily in the south of England. Chilham is also a friendly place of old redbrick and flint stone houses around a Norman church. In the churchyard is the fenced off stump of an ancient yew tree which was about 1300 years old. Unfortunately during the storm of October 1987 it had been destroyed by nearby trees falling on to it. I remembered that storm, I had been living in Maidstone and the fir trees next door were snapped off at six foot. Entire woods were flattened to the ground. There is a tiny post office in Chilham but it did not open for half an hour so I enquired if there was a shop nearby and was given some vague directions to a farm shop some distance away on the main road. Walking a little way and seeing no signs for a shop I decided to wait for the post office to open. There wasn't much food but I bought two chocolate bars and a ring pull can of macaroni which I ate cold for my first break. I bought a postcard for my eldest daughter as she has a collection of all the postcards sent to her over the years. The post office counter was not yet open so the nice lady gave me one of her own stamps for free. We discussed the threatened solar farm, no one was happy about it (except I presume the land owner). She also felt too many new houses were being built in the area as well.

"It's because of all these immigrants coming over" she said, a rather prejudiced comment but that was how she felt.

The day remained misty as I followed the North Downs Way through coppiced woodland and over muddy fields of broad beans where no path had been left. At one point joining with the E2 trans-Europe footpath route. A particularly long section over a broad bean field was made worse with the thick mist obscuring the end. As I slithered and slipped through the tacky mud I felt the name was rather a misnomer, I was not on the *Downs* Way but below the Downs on the *Mud* Way. I was becoming traumatised with the mud.

In a rather non-descript village the only interest was wondering why the houses had been given the names they had; 'Caithness' in Kent? Was 'Trevone' derived from a combination of Simone and Trevor? 'Dunroamin' and 'Rose Cottage' were just unoriginal. Enroute to Charing the land became increasingly bleak with dull woodland, vast ploughed fields, muddy tracks and the background noise of the M20. Charing itself is an attractive village with a mixture of red-brick and flint faced houses with old red tiled roofs. There were toilets, a good shop and for some reason three policemen standing on the pavement, a fact everyone was discussing as no one knew why they were there. The helpful lady in the shop filled my water bottle and I stocked up with food. Towards the end of each day there was a daily search for drinking water, in the mountains this is never a problem as there are fresh streams you can drink from. Public toilets have wash units you cannot get water from and public taps are non-existent. Liquids weigh one kilogram per litre and so I only carried a 500ml flask of hot water during the day.

I was tired as I hunted for somewhere to camp above Lenham. On the common there was ideal short grass but I was nervous to camp where people were out dog walking.

I found a corner of a field tucked out of sight behind some woods. It was not the best site, I had to trample down dead vegetation and remove some brambles to clear a space, and the field I stepped out on to was muddy. If it had been later in my walk I would have happily camped in view but I was also aware that it is not officially legal to 'wild camp' in England. There was the noise of traffic and some nearby construction work, also random gunshots at times which was disconcerting. I couldn't locate where they were coming from and someone was still shooting in the morning so I wore my headtorch when I set out. I didn't really want to get shot in my first week of the walk, would have been rather annoying. On mentioning this to my son he said that the gunshots were probably the sound of automatic bird scarers!

The next day I dropped down early into Lenham which is well served with a co op, café, pub and post office. Passing an estate agents I glanced at the prices, most houses were over £600,000 and even a 1970's estate three-bed semi was £330,000. How does anyone afford these prices? On the Isle of Lewis this would buy a detached house with land. Walking up through the village the noise of the M20 increased until it really was intolerable and yet there was an estate of new large detached houses right beside it. One house even had an Aston Martin parked on the driveway along with two other cars. Now if I could afford that I wouldn't buy a house next to the M20. Crossing the motorway the noise was less and I realised the noise had been so intense my ears popped! A sign said no to 5,000 more houses nearby.

Near Ulcombe I joined the Greensand Way and sat in the churchyard to eat some bread. Throughout the south I stopped in churchyards as they provided an escape from the traffic and usually contained benches, in this case there were two folding chairs by the door. An ancient yew tree grew nearby, this one not destroyed in the 1987 storm. Ulcombe is the first in a line of ancient churches built on the 100 metre contour overlooking the Weald of Kent.

I was heading for the southern edge of Maidstone to return to where I lived from June 1985 until November 1989 and the Greensand Way would conveniently take me there. It was the most enjoyable section of my walk so far, passing through orchards and along quiet roads, good views over the weald to the hazy ridge of the High Weald. The sun shone in a blue sky and I was back in an area I used to cycle through. It was good to see how little it had changed and how it would still be pleasant to cycle through. I waited while one hundred and thirty goats walked ahead in to a field, it was 'Buttercups goat sanctuary'. There is an amazing variety of goats, they come in all colours and sizes, though one looked suspiciously like a Soay sheep! I did wonder where all these goats come from, presumably rehomed from elsewhere in Britain.

I ate lunch in Boughton Monchelsea churchyard overlooking the deer park. I had often sat on the same bench when I lived nearby but had no recollection of the fallow deer, there were over one hundred soaking in the warmth of the sun. My memory was of the pink valerian flowers which grew out of the wall in the summer, a plant I had never seen before.

Exiting Linton park on to the A229 on the outskirts of Maidstone I was struck by the full bombardment of traffic. I had lodged in a bungalow beside the A229, it was definitely not as busy in 1985 and is now more built up. I changed into trainers as I would be road walking, they felt light and bouncy compared to walking boots. I tried to find the house where I had stayed but I couldn't remember the number and did not recognise anywhere, even though I had walked up and down the road to work daily. I had spent a year working in a home for two autistic young adults, we had taken them to the village church in Loose nearby. An extremely steep hill leads down to the village and the church, an old metal sign warns charabancs and carriages of the steepness of the hill! We had sat in the pews near the back of the church. The back pew had been where the men from a home for ex-alcoholics sat, they had eaten sweets during the lengthy sermons. The pews have gone and have been replaced by chairs giving a more flexible, useable space.

A stream runs through the valley and it is possible to follow it to Tovil where I moved to afterwards. I couldn't remember the route so had to ask the way, it is attractive and rural compared to the busy roads nearby. Somewhere amongst rough land back in 1985 there used to be a lion kept in a large cage, you could hear it roaring as you went past which was always unsettling. I did wonder if my memory was wrong as now it seems crazy someone could keep a lion like that but there are lots of accounts from others about it online.

Tovil has lots more houses than in the 1980's and I was pleased to come across a Lidl, I could shop and buy bakery goodies. I had for a while lodged in a large house in Tovil, there had been a family of six and three lodgers all sharing one bathroom. It is now deluxe ensuite bedsits, changing times. A footpath follows the river Medway which looked dull coloured and slow moving. A tarmac path took me to my final destination that day of East Farleigh a little way west along the river. I don't remember ever walking along the river this way, perhaps I didn't have the time or possibly it wasn't safe then. Kent in the mid-80's had seen more than its fair share of random attacks and murders of women, it had not always felt the safest place to be. It did feel quite gloomy initially beside the river as there were steep wooded slopes each side and the sun had disappeared. House boats were moored up, areas of land between the river and the railway line taken over for gardens and woodsheds and all the usual paraphernalia associated with boats. One boat had goats and chickens on their plot of land. In 1989 I had rented a static caravan in East Farleigh for seven months, in an escape from the student nurses' home! It had been a small, half empty site beside the river, near the railway station and level crossing. The crossing is now controlled remotely but then there was a signal man who would open and close large wooden gates. The early morning trains used to rattle the crockery but it was a lovely site with views through the trees of the river. The trees are gone and now it is the Empress Riverside Park with electronic gates and over one hundred park homes. I sat outside the pub with a beer and a packet of cheesy biscuits watching the cars queuing to cross the railway and then the river, there was a long wait as the river bridge is narrow and becomes a bottleneck.

I continued along the riverside path which is tarmac and well used, I missed the old meandering, earth path and the trees but it is now much more accessible. My plan was to camp in a meadow about a mile further on, but a 'private, no footpath' sign rather stopped that. It was dusk and I didn't want to go any further so I found an empty corner of a churchyard and put my tent up. The only complaints were from the scolding blackbirds. Foxes fighting gave noise to the night and stars shone.

The next day was my 59th birthday, it is not every year that you wake up on your birthday in a churchyard! I celebrated with milky coffee and two chocolate croissants for breakfast then set off as soon as it was light enough to walk. The moon was still out and a frost had formed as I walked through orchards to the road. A jogger went past and early morning dog-walkers. The road was busy and built-up, a vape shop proclaimed that vaping is 95%

safer than smoking?! I was going to see the hospital where I trained as a nurse in 1986-89 and the student nurses' home. I arrived first at the site of the old psychiatric hospital which was in the process of being closed down in the 1980's. The vast Victorian buildings have been converted into luxury apartments, I couldn't believe the extent of the buildings. When I lived in the nurses' home opposite I think most of the buildings were empty and off-limits but there was a long corridor linking different buildings that we would walk through. Dickensian figures loitered in this corridor, patients who had been interned there for years, some since world-war two. One man was always begging for a light and there was a lady who clutched a doll, images that have always stayed imprinted on my mind. These long-stay patients were housed in old 'nightingale' style wards, each patient allocated a bed and a locker for their few belongings. I wondered if the ghosts of the past still haunted the buildings, I certainly would not like to live there. Questioning a man who lives in the converted chapel, he said it was a lovely place to live and most residents were not around in the 1980's to have seen the hospital. It had also been derelict for almost thirty years so good to be renovated. The surrounding grounds are very pleasant with trees and the old high wall keeps it hidden from busy traffic. The sheer scale of the site though and the thought of the thousands who had passed through the building made me cry.

Across the road the student nurses' home is gone, replaced by flats and houses. The hospital is still there but no longer standing amongst fields, more houses are being built nearby immediately next to the busy road and I became confused with a new road unmarked on my map. I was heading to East Malling which meant crossing a field with a 'beware of the bull' notice. I am never too sure what as a walker you are supposed to do, but said bull wasn't present so that was a relief.

Reaching East Malling I stopped in the churchyard. An old plaque high up by the church door is inscribed

"nearby lyeth the body of Mary Barker
Buried Dec 4 1753 at the advanced age of 105"

One hundred and five! I thought about that as I continued on my way, was her age an error or had she really lived to such an age? If so how come she had not been accused of being a witch? The plaque also only says *advanced* age, not *incredible* or *unique* age. Who was she? Researching about her when I returned home has revealed nothing, she is not even mentioned in the guide to the church. I find this strange, the fact that someone lived so long is amazing to me. As I got lost in the housing estates I thought how the current residents of the area were very unlikely to live to such an age judging by their appearance and the proximity of so many busy roads. The minor road on my map I wanted to walk is now a dual-carriage way leading to the motorway!

At the village of Leybourne is the site of the old British Legion hospital where I carried out my first ward experience. It was a surgical orthopaedic ward and the only one still left in the hospital at the time! I think it closed down shortly afterwards and transferred to the new hospital. A whole new community has been built on the site, pleasant houses and a new school with woods and level tarmac paths. Quite ideal except it is next to the M20 and the noise was loud and must be constant. In the old churchyard I sat on a bench in the sun, a plaque announced it was in memory of Cathy Jones

'memories of your cheerfulness will never fade. Love from your friends'
15.10.57-22.09.92

What a lovely epitaph. I crossed the motorway bridge to Ryarsh where more homes were being built, some with French doors, though I wondered if they would ever be opened. It was noisy. A little further on the old village was quiet and peaceful and the lane led to Coldrum Long Barrow, a 4,000 BC neolithic burial chamber. I remembered it as being on the actual downs but memories can be wrong. It is actually beside ploughed fields below the hills, not such an auspicious location as many burial chambers.

I re-joined the North Downs Way which follows the old Pilgrims' route to Canterbury below the downs. Badgers have dug their homes in the bank sending chalk and clay down on to the road. The church of Trottiscliffe is strangely in a hollow so that bizarrely only the top of the tower shows peeping up out of the surrounding fields. At Wrotham I hoped to find toilets and water and saw a 'welcome' sign outside the church but below was a list of do's and don'ts relating to covid;

"use the hand sanitiser, wear a mask, do not sit on a pew, only sit on the plastic chairs and if you do, place a used sign on it afterwards, and try not to touch anything"!

I did not feel very welcome. I also confess I did touch the door handles to the toilet and the kitchen, both were locked.

From my camp spot in old woods up on the North Downs that night I could see a multitude of red lights marking the tops of cranes in London. I watched the sun set orange to the drone of the M20 and realised that barely any of Kent had been out of the sound of traffic and motorways.

It was still rural as I walked through Knatts valley the next morning, 1930's bungalows line the road before arriving at large ploughed fields. The bungalows have such names as 'Hillview', 'Foxwood', 'Woodland', 'Ivydale' and the rather confusing 'Moorings', there is no water around. Reaching Farningham I was glad to see a family butchers and bought a large slice of pork and egg pie. It is an attractive village of old red brick and flint faced houses with a clear river and gardens, one yellow with aconites. It is below the M20 with an underpass to access the woods which are a nature reserve (opened in 1986 by David Attenborough).

Nearer to London the city encroached on the countryside with rubbish lining the roads. A field entrance was blocked with fly tipping, pity the poor farmer who will have to clear it away to be able to plant his field. I followed a mixture of roads, footpaths and parks through the edge of London to reach the suburbs of Bexley and Welling where my step-nan had lived. I was revisiting some of my earliest memories.

Chapter 3

London to Hitchin – early memories, canals and old ways

21st-26th January

I arrived at Danson park, Welling, in time for lunch. Mum had brought my sister and myself here when we were little. It is a large pleasant park, I sat in the rose garden and ate the pie bought in Farningham, it was good. Nearby was the old house which is now the registry office. Until I started planning this trip I thought it was *Damson* park as in the plums, I had visions of lots of plum trees. It was quite disappointing to discover it is in fact *Danson* park. The estate was evidently known as Densynton in the late 13th century and then by 1327 as Danston, nothing to do with plums at all.

I needed to find Farnham road where my step-nan and grandad had lived. My grandad died when I was four and I sadly have no memory of him. The house was one of many 1930's three-bed semi's with the large bay window in the front room which was only used for visitors. As a child I had always worried how mum would find her way there among all the identical roads and houses. Walking there now I could still see why I had been worried, there were so many streets of similar houses. When my sister Sarah, who is two years older than me and I were pre-school mum would take us to stay there for a few days, we would 'top and tail' on a mattress on the floor in the smallest bedroom. The toilet was at the top of the high, straight staircase, I found it scary. At home our toilet was in an out-building and our stairs were narrow and twisting. I did like the back doorstep, it was the perfect height for a small child to sit on. It was here, age three and half, that I learnt to knit with green plastic needles and royal blue wool. There was a large apple tree in the back garden. The front doorsill was highly polished brass, we were forbidden to step on it and had to jump across it!

Once we were older we just went for day visits arriving in time for lunch, which was invariably boiled bacon and potatoes on big white plates. Afterwards we would go next-door where mum's aunt Ada lived with her brother-in-law, uncle Alf. It was slightly confusing as they had both been married (aunt Ada in fact to another Alf) and moved in together for company when their respective spouses died. Aunt Ada had helped bring mum up and her three boys had been like mum's brothers as she was an only child. Mum was very fond of aunt Ada, whereas I think she visited her step-mum out of duty. My maternal grandmother had died when mum was fourteen and grandad had remarried a year later, it cannot have been easy for mum.

I liked these visits to aunt Ada and uncle Alf. Uncle Alf would be sitting in his rocking chair watching 'the magic roundabout' on the small black and white television. He always had a pipe in his mouth, I am not sure it was ever lit.

As we left aunt Ada would hand Sarah and me some money which we had to refuse initially and then we could take it. Mum said it was wrong to just take the money as though we wanted it. I thought that was confusing as I did want it!

Sometimes we would meet old friends of mum's who lived in that part of London. There was 'auntie' Elsie (we addressed all adults as aunt or uncle if we knew their first name) who had beautiful thick, brown, curly hair. She seemed quite exotic to me. There was also 'auntie' Stephie who was older than mum and had a sad past as she had escaped from former Yugoslavia. She had left her country and never seen her son or husband again, it sounded quite 'romantic' to me as a child but thinking now it was just tragic.

Eventually everyone ended up in residential homes which I remember visiting once as a teenager. Mum I think managed a few visits but as we didn't own a car it wasn't an easy journey, entailing a bus to our station and several trains to and across London. Mum's ill-health meant her visits were very infrequent and she was not well enough to even attend her step-mum's funeral. I remember she did go to aunt Ada's funeral where she met her cousins and relatives for the last time as after that she had no connections to her London life.

After finding the house I headed to the station and caught trains west to Barnes where I had arranged to stay with my eldest niece, Anna and her fiancé, Ricky. I was glad of the chance to rest and think about the first week of my walk. Kent had been much harder than expected with the combination of the mud and the motorway noise, also the many changes since I lived there. It is always a shock leaving the quiet of the island and I was still adjusting to being amongst so many people and buildings.

My feet were hurting from the pavements, I had some

concern over pain in the ball of my right foot. Hopefully it would resolve itself but I was worried that perhaps I couldn't do the walk, had I been conceited to think I could walk so far? There was though a sense of satisfaction too that I had completed the first section of my walk within the time scale I had planned. I had walked all the way from the coast to London. I tried not to think of the walk as a whole but to focus on each section, or even each day, as to think of the walk in its entirety was overwhelming.

I arrived at Anna's on a Friday in order to run Richmond Park parkrun the next day. Ricky kindly dropped us off and we waited for runners to arrive at the start point. I squeezed in to the start funnel along with over four hundred other parkrunners. I wasn't too sure about the covid safety of such a 'cosy' start and felt slightly daunted at the number of people, I was used to rather fewer runners. The 'pep' talk touched on covid safety too with the reminder of 'no spitting'! Everyone soon spread out once we set off on the three mile loop of the park. We ran to the accompaniment of parakeets making it seem like a safari park! It was a straight forward course, though I held back for the two hills we were warned about towards the end – I was still waiting for them as I finished! I didn't get such a quick time as the week before but was pleased to be 25th female out of 150 females.

Anna and I strolled back through the park to Barnes passing red deer and old gnarled trees. Richmond Park is very extensive and with the trees and absence of traffic noise you could be miles from London. I vaguely knew the park as I had come here with my girls when we had lived in Sunbury-on-Thames for a year in 1996. Later Anna drove me there so I could visit the house we had lived in. It was another 1930's three bed semi on a very quiet road, so quiet in fact that the two oldest would play on the pavement aged two and three. They favoured a spot by the neighbour's wall which for some obscure reason they called 'the pig stile'. I had not enjoyed living in Sunbury but it is a very pleasant place. We walked down to the river Thames where we used to go to feed the ducks, and through the park stopping to admire the millennium tapestry, an impressive piece of community embroidery.

Anna fed me well too, even producing a birthday cake, I was not sure when someone had last baked me a birthday cake. I am used to home cooking and fresh vegetables from our own land as well as our own eggs from hens and ducks, so had been finding processed camp food rather basic. It also very much depended upon what local shops had to offer. I found that a lot of village shops in the south of England were poorly stocked with proper food, I would enter and be met by a wall of sweets and round the corner aisles of alcohol, fizzy drinks and crisps. Further north the shops improved, I found the further a place was from big towns the better the local shop would be.

I left Anna and Ricky's on the Sunday morning feeling rested and well fed. I had clean clothes and my feet felt good. I wore my trainers and was excited to be on my way again and heading North on my walk. My next destination was Enfield in north east London where I had lived when first married in 1989 until moving to Norfolk in 1992.

Having no intention of walking across London I caught trains to Bethnal Green from where it was a short walk to the Lea valley, going first through Victoria Park. It seemed like the equivalent of the population of Stornoway were out at 9am on the Sunday morning running, cycling and dog walking, I had never seen a park so busy. But crossing over the A102(M) via a footbridge I entered a world of graffiti on White Post Lane, albeit that some of it was quite artistic. I felt rather vulnerable as no one was around, but soon met the Lea Valley navigation where everyone was out walking.

This was to be the first Sunday of several that I would be walking along a canal past houseboats with logs, sacks of coal, bicycles, buggies and flower tubs on their roofs. They are home to people but their existence is under threat as the city council wants to remove five hundred and fifty moorings to make room for more leisure sports. Many houseboats were already illegally moored. A protest was organised later on in the year in an attempt to save their homes.

It was about mid-day when I reached Lea Bridge road from where it was a short walk to Walthamstow and lunch with my sister-in-law, Judith and her husband. Afterwards Judith accompanied me through Walthamstow marshes to Tottenhale where I re-joined the Lea valley walk. The area was busy yet an urban fox trotted along the path unafraid of the people. The marshes have only recently been made open to the public and during lock-down the paths were so busy that a one-way system had to be introduced. North East London is a densely populated area with terraces of houses and maisonettes so any open spaces are heavily used. The Lea valley is a great outdoor space there.

I continued walking along the canal, several barges were heading towards London. One barge passed by full of sacks of coal and logs, presumably to deliver to people living on the canal, a massive dog sat on the top. Two women were wheeling their chemi-loos to empty them, the 'delight' of living on a boat. I had booked to stay at a campsite at Picket Lock for the night as I thought it would be risky just camping out but as the canal became quieter and the afternoon drew on I wasn't so sure. It felt very unsafe leaving the canal to get to the campsite past piles of rubbish and suspiciously occupied parked cars. I presume they were drug dealing and hurried past hoping to be invisible. The campsite was also very quiet, I was the only tent (a couple of caravans were in another section) and the office closed at 4pm. It would probably have been just as safe to camp on a rough area of ground. But the only disturbances at night were the sounds of fighting foxes and my mind wondering if they would have the audacity to break into the tent for food. It was the only time I felt unsafe camping on the walk.

The next day I caught a bus to Enfield as I did not want to walk miles through streets. It was the school bus so soon became full of surprisingly subdued school children. I got off at Gordon Hill station, we had lived nearby in a flat which looked just the same as I remembered from 1989. It was comforting after all the changes I had found in Maidstone, but I didn't recall the walk down to the house we later moved to even though it was a route I walked to and from work. The house and road also looked as I remembered, a row of twenty terraced houses each side of a dead-end road.

I walked round the corner to Forty Hall Park which is on the very edge of Enfield. I glanced in an estate agents window and saw lots of houses for over one million pounds and wondered how anyone affords to buy property there. Near the red brick 'dolls house' style Forty Hall grows a large Cedar of Lebanon. A plaque proudly states it's three hundred and fifty years old and probably the oldest specimen in Britain. It's an interesting trait that any plaque will claim that the object of interest is the oldest, biggest, most complete etc.. in the country. It would be lovely to see a plaque just saying that something is an interesting old ruin or tree with no claims to anything.

I took the road out through Crews Hill into Hertfordshire. In 1989 it was an area of glasshouses and I cycled out to a 'pick your own' strawberry place putting the punnets in my panniers to go home and make jam. Now there is an array of garden, plant, aquatic and knick-knack shops, one place promising an exciting visit! (I wasn't quite sure what they sold or what that meant!) An animal feed place advertises their dog washrooms where you can wash and groom your dog. The pictures showed beautifully clean dogs and I thought of our unkempt bearded collie and imagined him emerging transformed. Dogs are well catered for, nearby is a dog day-care centre 'to meet all your dogs' needs'. Half a dozen vans were parked outside, presumably they drive round and collect dogs daily, a 'doggy school bus'.

At Cuffley I shopped for food and bought some soft insoles to cushion my right foot which was feeling painful again from the roads. Large detached houses line the road which leads to the woods, new houses infilling between older houses. I noted all the new houses have electronic gates but not the original houses. A house being built, squeezing in between two older houses, boasted five bedrooms, cinema room, wine room and gym!

When I was ten I had camped with my primary school in Cuffley woods and loved it but when I got home and found mum I had burst into tears. "Didn't you enjoy it?" she had asked. I had never been away without a family member before so it was just the emotion of seeing her again. Also other children had been met off the bus by their parents but as we always walked ourselves to school it had not occurred to mum to meet me.

Later I followed the Hertfordshire Way along old by-roads with no mud and little noise. I wrote in my diary that it was idyllic, it was so dry I had walked all day in trainers. The only thing I did note were all the 'private, keep-out' signs on field openings and gates, one area of woodland even had signs announcing guard dogs on patrol. There were also notices warning of regular police patrols to catch poachers and hare coursers. I presume it was the problem of being so close to London and other urban areas. I knocked on the door of an old house to ask for water. An elderly man came to the door and I explained I had knocked there as they didn't have electronic gates, unlike most of the houses. He sighed and said a house nearby had sold for over four million pounds!

In Essendon for the first time I camped in plain view of anyone who might come along the footpath as I tucked my tent in the corner of a meadow. I was at the back of some gardens and it felt very safe as the Hertfordshire villages were quiet and wealthy. It appeared only wealthy people could afford to live in them and I was surprised to find a foodbank collection box in the church porch. I presume it is to take to the poor in nearby towns such as Welwyn or Hatfield where the families live and there are large housing estates. A verse of 'All things bright and beautiful' kept running through my head;

"The rich man in his castle, the poor man at his gate
He made them high and lowly
He ordered their estate"

The sense of entitlement those Victorian hymn writers had still holds true nowadays.

It was a quiet night, just the screech of owls and the early morning mewings of red kites. The latter are a newer addition to the area, when I was growing up red kites were extremely rare birds. It was with some satisfaction I packed up thinking how probably no one in the houses nearby knew I had camped there. It was a lovely days walking following the Lea valley way and Hertfordshire way. The birds were awakening as I set off and I saw a fox.

Initially the route negotiated the South Herts towns of Hatfield and Welwyn, at one point going under the motorway. The underpass was so low I had to duck and walkers share it with the river Lea. Judging by the amount of debris in the tunnel walkers must have to wade through the water at times. The streams now were clear with stony beds. Welwyn has a pleasant linear park with a lake where you can hire pedalos and rowing boats. There were lots of water birds too; cormorant, heron, coots and little egrets.

I stopped in the attractive village of Wheathampsted for lunch eating a sausage baguette on a bench outside the bakers and watching the world go by. Genteel elderly ladies went into the old-fashioned pharmacy while outside a young staff member was smoking. Lycra clad cyclists stopped to buy food and drink at the bakers and mothers with young children chatted outside.

Old lanes continued to Ayot St Lawrence, they were quiet and, apart from some bad fly tipping and a burnt out car at the start, rubbish free. I have a photo of my sister in front of the ruined church in Ayot St Lawrence taken over forty years ago when we had cycled from home there. I attempted to replicate the photo with a selfie and of course minus the bicycles. It took rather a few attempts before I had succeeded in getting myself and the church in the photo! The church is a ruin as in the eighteenth century a new Greek style church was built in the village and the old church closed. It was then robbed of some stones before it was deliberately ruined in the early nineteenth century for the 'romantic' effect. It is also the location of George Bernard Shaw's house, now a National Trust property. I have to confess that forty years ago I didn't know who he was and I still have yet to read his works.

I was back in my old cycling area. As a teenager I would cycle for miles through North Hertfordshire at weekends and it was lovely to discover that it is still very quiet and unchanged. I camped at the edge of St Paul's Warden on some rough ground. I had contemplated staying in the churchyard which is very large and partly empty but a local lady felt that some people might object. As I ate my dinner

I heard the church bells start to ring, initially it was just two bells so obviously people learning. I rang church bells for years though I haven't rung for about eight years but I thought it would be good to go along if they had a proper practise night. I lay down and listened as a few more bells began to ring and thought if I heard at least four bells ringing I would go along......the next thing I knew all was quiet, I looked at my watch, it was 9.30pm! I had fallen asleep so if there had been bell-ringing practise I had slept right through it, I will never know.

As I set out the next morning there was a pale pink sunrise. The weather had been overcast and still since before London, quite monotonous, some sunshine would make a change. I enjoyed starting out just as it was getting light each day, listening to the birds singing and seeing animals. That morning I saw roe and muntjac deer, a hare as well as buzzards and red kite.

I walked past the Sue Ryder home at Stagenhoe which triggered a childhood memory from when I was about seven. Back then at the end of the 1960's it had been a home for old Polish folk and a group of us children had been taken there near Christmas to play our recorders wearing fairy dresses. I remember handing out bowls of sweets too.

I followed the Hertfordshire Way past a ruined Minsden chapel in the middle of ploughed fields, it had been built from the flint stones gathered off the land. In a neighbouring field there were piles of flint stones at the edge, presumably removed from the field. I wasn't sure if that would be by hand or by machine, I know in Herefordshire migrant workers were employed to stone pick. Crossing a busy dual-carriageway near Stevenage, I could see the hospital where my father had spent his last few weeks following a massive stroke. The land became more open with big fields but there were some old meadows with falling down ancient trees on the approach to Great Wymondley. There I discovered a wonderful array of homemade jams and chutneys for sale in the church porch to raise money for essential repairs. It was a shame I couldn't really carry any, some jam would have made a welcome addition to my menu. There was also a large selection of books people can take for a donation.

I reached the edge of Hitchin, it was our nearest town when I was a child and where I attended secondary school. I hadn't enjoyed school so deliberately avoided visiting it on my walk. I was heading to the station as I was going to make a detour to Norfolk and return to where I had lived in the 1990's.

Chapter 4

Norfolk; sun and space

26th-28th January

I caught a train to Cambridge where I had nearly an hour to wait for the train to King's Lynn. It was nice to just sit and rest and write my diary. I had noticed a poster near Great Wymondley advertising a meeting against the proposed green-belt solar farm nearby, yet another development on agricultural land in the south. I thought about the wording of solar *farms*. It is an interesting use of the word farm as it makes the construction of them seem less destructive on farmland, yet they render the land unproductive for food. The Oxford dictionary definition of the word farm is 'an area of land......for growing crops, rearing animals etc.' I am all for green energy but I do feel that it isn't the solution to put solar farms on good land and I would like to see a word other than *farm* used to denote them (ditto with wind farms). Approaching Ely I saw extensive solar panels on one side of the train track and on the other side vast fields of grass being grown for turf. Large machines were busy rolling up 'turf carpets' leaving the ground bare and vulnerable to wind and rain erosion.

Ceasing my ranting, the train ride from Cambridge to King's Lynn is lovely travelling through the flat open fenland with far reaching views. The sun shone in a blue sky and it was relaxing watching the fields and houses go by. I was amused to see how much the telegraph poles lean, I had forgotten about the 'fen lean', a result of the land reclaimed from the sea drying out. Farmhouses abandoned due to too much subsidence sit in the middle of treeless fields.

I sat in the sun on a park bench in King's Lynn before catching a bus east to Necton where we lived from June 1992 until November 1995. It is a large village surrounded by arable fields in the Breckland area of Norfolk. My three girls had been born while we lived there, the youngest at home the other two in King's Lynn hospital. We would catch the old double decker buses that went between Norwich and King's Lynn passing Necton road end. I was surprised to get on a very modern bus; they are now wheelchair accessible, have wifi, USB points and you can press a little button for a coat hook to pop out! Plus an electronic voice announces each stop, which was just as well as I barely recognised the Necton stop. There used to be a small fish and chip shop there but now there is a large garage with a co op, drive-through Costa Coffee and new houses.

It's a short walk from the main road into the village where I stopped first to look in the church, a large perpendicular flint stone church approached up an avenue of severely bollarded trees. I had forgotten the amazing carved wooden ceiling of angels and saints, typical of this part of Norfolk. I walked along to the well-stocked shop to buy some milk. The butchers next-door were advertising pheasants for £2 and partridge for £1, they would have been good but I wasn't sure I would be able to butcher one with my knife let alone cook one on my small stove. I continued to where we had lived, an unattractive 1970's chalet bungalow now with a bright pink painted garage door. Necton has lots of housing estates, the close next door is of bungalows which always had a holiday chalet feel with their gable ends facing the road.

I wanted space so headed out on a quiet road through fields to the wonderfully named hamlet of Ivy Todd. It was where we had often walked and, in the autumn picked blackberries. My eldest daughter had even named a knitted doll Ivy Todd, she still has it almost thirty years later! There were more houses than I remembered but there must have always been that many as none were new. It was hard to find somewhere to camp, in the end I trampled down dead vegetation at the edge of a field and tucked myself out of sight. It wasn't a very peaceful night as I could hear traffic on the main road and in the evening military planes roared overhead. Necton is used as a landmark for planes from the nearby American airbase at Lakenheath. Russia was threatening to invade the Ukraine, perhaps they were practising in readiness to get involved.

On my way to catch an early bus in the morning I picked up a free book from a book 'cupboard' outside a house. I found a few of these 'libraries' throughout Britain located in old red telephone boxes, bus shelters, church porches or as in Ivy Todd purpose made boxes. I think many of them sprung up during and after the covid-19 lockdown when public libraries were closed and folk had time to read a lot. They are a great idea and I hope they remain. I hadn't been carrying a book to keep the weight of my pack down so it was good to be able to find a book on a non-walking day. It was Richard Mabe's account of moving from the Chilterns to East Anglia. It seemed appropriate as I was heading to the edge of the Chiltern Hills where I grew up.

I waited for the bus back to King's Lynn by a very busy A47, school children travelling towards Norwich have to cross the road to wait for their bus. There isn't a crossing so they dodge over when there is a brief gap in the traffic, not easy and I wondered when an accident will happen. I wasn't sad to be leaving Necton, I had never been very fond of the area and now it was so much noisier.

I got off the bus at Southgate, one of the old medieval entrances to King's Lynn and walked through old houses to South Lynn where we had lived over the winter of 1995. On the way in to the town I noticed that the Campbell soup factory was no longer there and now there was an absence of the associated smell which used to pervade that area. The road to South Lynn has been enlarged and new houses built and the massive old factory which overshadowed the small terrace housing is gone. I found my way to Atbara terrace where we had lived, a small dead-end road with a single row of red brick terrace houses on one side. It looked as it did in 1995, small old houses with the addition now of green wheelie-bins.

Walking back past old terrace houses in to town and wandering round the medieval area made me feel quite touristy in the sunshine. There are some very interesting buildings, many suffering from subsidence with windows at odd angles and bulging walls. The great end gable of St Mary's church leans precariously over the street and another building had metal bars propping it up over the gap between the adjacent house! King's Lynn is not a wealthy area and the housing is some of the poorest I saw. A lot of the housing is eighteenth century with old single glazed windows and looks damp and in poor repair. It is a very interesting historic town but it is out on a limb and not somewhere to go on holiday.

I caught a mid-day bus out to Wiggenhall St Germans, a small village on the edge of the fens beside the river Great Ouse. We had lived there from May 1997 until September

1998. The sun shone in a cloudless sky though there was a cold wind as I sat in the churchyard to eat lunch. When I popped into the church I discovered it was the best church I had been in as everything was unlocked. I was able to use the toilet and fill up my water bottle in the kitchen. I was impressed with the facilities as we had attended the church and then the 'toilet' had been a chemical porta-potti behind a curtain in the side-chapel! There had also not been a kitchen or running water. The only 'water' had been the puddles on the stone floor which rose up after heavy rain due to the fact that the church is lower than the level of the river! (I think they still suffer from that problem).

My plan was to walk out and camp in a meadow where we had a picnic on my youngest daughter's third birthday some twenty-four years ago. It was beside what is known in the area as a 'drain' which is a man-made river for keeping the fens drained and there are sluice gates to control the water levels. These sluice gates were near Wiggenhall St Mary's and so are known as St Mary's sluice and they were quite small, we had often walked by them enroute to the nearby village. Before my trip my son had joked that there would now be a factory or some such development on the meadow, to which I had replied it was very unlikely. On reaching the last fence before the sluice I came to a notice forbidding unauthorised access and a big new sluice construction! How true he spoke.

I walked to the redundant church in the village of St Mary's instead and tucked my tent into a corner of the churchyard. It was a good spot, the grass was flat and my tent caught the evening sun. It was very peaceful, apart from a grey squirrel in the tree above dropping bits down onto my tent. After my initial disappointment about the meadow by the sluice I realised that nothing stays the same. The sense of space with the wide open skies in the fens was still there though.

Morning dawned with a thick mist creating an atmospheric scene with the reeds and the birds on the water as I returned to St Germans. I passed the small village school which my oldest had attended. Next door is the playing field and village hall where I had taken the other two to mums and toddlers. There is now a post office in a tiny cubbyhole at the side of the hall. I wanted to post some maps home so waited until 9am for it to open. Asking the lady if she had any large envelopes I was told in no uncertain terms that she was a post office and did not do retail and I needed to go to the shop for an envelope! When I returned later, having bought an envelope at the shop I was tempted to suggest she changed jobs if she was unhappy but then thought she might not post my parcel, so kept quiet!

Passing the tiny 'two-up, two-down' terrace house we had lived in, I returned to the church again as I had seen there was a coffee morning advertised. Entering the building the heavy door banged shut and my walking poles clattered as they slipped off the wooden pew I leant them against. A lady came over and asked quietly if I had come for the prayer meeting, I replied I was there for the coffee morning! The notice had said 'Friday 9.30am coffee morning', nothing about prayers first and it was gone that time. A lady dusting the pews came and chatted, the pew ends are elaborately carved with people and strange animals. They are late medieval and quite quirky, she said that some represent the seven deadly sins and were warnings for the parishioners. There are some animals/people in rather uncompromising poses. Prayers over I was made welcome, there was coffee and cake, it was someone's birthday. I was surprised to meet Margaret who remembered me and the girls from 1997, and after talking a while I even remembered her too.

I felt sad to leave St Germans as I had enjoyed living there and it is really rather beautiful sitting both sides of the River Ouse with a mixture of houses. There is an old stone bridge over the river and high levees built to contain the river. The whole area is though at risk of flooding and I remember when we lived there the flood sirens sounding for practise. The instructions were to stay put, fill up containers with water and move upstairs. I wasn't sure what people in bungalows were supposed to do. There had been bad flooding the year we lived there but we were down river to the flood gates and so were alright; the gates protect the villages and King's Lynn but result in the farmland upstream to them being flooded. When roads re-opened we had driven and seen farm houses still marooned on their tiny 'islands'.

A signpost by the river indicated King's Lynn five and a half miles away so I decided to walk, the girls had been too young to walk that far when we lived there. It was a surprisingly pleasant walk following the river Great Ouse. The sun burnt through the mist, water droplets shimmered on the reeds and cormorants perched on posts spreading their wings to dry. At another sluice, which the path crosses I jumped as a robotic voice announced 'this is an automatic structure for your own safety keep to the footpath'. Now who in their right mind would climb on sluice gates especially as they are fenced off? The warning is announced again as you leave the sluice gates.

The sky line of King's Lynn came into view, the two towers of St Mary's Minster the most prominent feature which was a surprise as they aren't very visible when in town. The path became busy with runners and dog walkers. It goes above the houses in South Lynn, views of small backyards and winter allotments. Back in town I picked up a free newspaper, the headlines were about two unrelated murders the week before and a young person killed in a car crash. On a positive note a junior school hall had been given a make-over and was now a Harry Potter Hogwarts!

There was an advanced notice for a hog roast in February for one hundred homeless people, I wondered where they were all staying at the moment. There were pages of houses to buy but many of the people I saw in town did not look very prosperous. An old lady in pyjama bottoms and cut-off wellies shuffled past in the bus station.

My time-out on the detour was over, it was time to move on and continue my walk, I caught an evening train to Letchworth, ready for the parkrun there the next day.

Chapter 5

Hitchin to Great Gaddesden; walking through the past

29th-31st January

Camping on the outskirts of Letchworth on the edge of a rough field I could see the distinct towers of the former psychiatric hospital at Arlesley, another vast Victorian institution. They had also been visible from the village where I grew up, standing as a warning. It was where 'mad' people were sent I had heard as a child.

I had walked out to the northern edge of the town to be near the parkrun for the next day. A man walking his dog asked where I was off to, a question I had been asked before at the end of the day. I suppose a lone woman striding along with a large pack is intriguing. I tended to answer evasively often saying a destination further than I intended to go. He wanted to know where I had come from asking "Is this what you do, just walk and camp?" I wondered whether I looked like a tramp and explained that I had also stayed with friends, at which he laughed and seemed to imply I was cheating not always camping out!

Letchworth is the first garden city to have been built and still seemed to retain a lot of the pride that garden cities have. Several people were out in the evening sweeping their front paths, it seemed people cared about the place. Sadly the motor cyclists riding up and down the wide lanes on the edge of town did not feel the same, one even performed a wheelie across the middle of the farmer's field! The ground was very dry and hard, the fields bare. The land felt stark and dead with the bare trees and hawthorn scrubland. Trees have been planted by the 'green' lanes but they have outgrown their plastic guards which lie discarded on the ground. It is a shame no one takes the time to tidy them up.

I packed up early and walked to Grange Park for parkrun, meeting a lovely lady enroute. Suki also walks, recently going on treks in India, rather more exotic than my walk. We chatted about the island and how her son who works in London has become passionate about trees and disillusioned with his work in finance. We could have talked for longer but parkrun 'called'. Parkrun was friendly too and a nice two lap route round the edge of fields. All 24's for myself as I ran it in 24:24 and came 24th overall! I chatted to one of the volunteers, Jennifer whose husband was cycling the 'coast to coast'. They had planned to walk it together but then covid put a stop to that, I didn't like to ask why they were not both walking it now. Afterwards I headed for the station and a train to Hitchin to resume my walk. Leaving Hitchin station I could see that area of town had changed, my father had worked at Bowman's flour mill which had been opposite the station. It is now gone, replaced by a B&M and flats.

Heading out of town for the village of Pirton, where I grew up, I followed my nose through the housing estates and then stopped at the edge of fields; I could see a village where I thought Pirton should be but wasn't sure if I recognised it. There were lots of trees and new houses with wide green paths leading that way and many people out walking. I asked a runner if indeed it was Pirton in case somehow I had gone the wrong way. I still remember the village being exposed and bare after the elm trees were all felled in the 1970's due to Dutch elm disease. The footpaths to the village had also been miserable edges to ploughed fields and certainly not very walked. The number of people walking was surprising, especially groups of young adults. In our teens my sister and I, along with a friend would walk to Hitchin on a Saturday or in the holidays to go swimming and we would rarely meet anyone. Now on this Saturday morning there were people spread out walking the entire way.

It was a lovely walk with sky larks singing and so dry underfoot that I was still in trainers. My route went via Oughtonhead nature reserve which is beside the small river His. King Henry V111 is reputed to have fallen in the His when pole vaulting the river at Hitchin! A rather peculiar claim to fame especially as the river is so narrow, there must have been bridges. I spent many hours at Oughtonhead with my father, who was a keen bird watcher hoping to see a kingfisher, we never did. I like looking out for birds but don't have the patience to stand around with binoculars waiting for birds to come along. My father had spent his precious free time with binoculars, recording what he saw. He also sent in records of butterflies and flowers. I am more of a bird spotter as I enjoy seeing them as I walk along. I am sorry I never learnt all the names of plants and birds from my father, he knew them all. My parents took us to paddle in the river at Oughtonhead when we were very young and when we were slightly older other friends would come along too, mum happily making a picnic large enough for everyone. Long-horn cattle now graze the areas of tall grass and reeds and the river is full of vegetation.

Growing up in the 1960's and 70's I had seen the spread of 'prairie' farming with the removal of hedges and the creation of vast fields, ploughed right to the edges. A recurring theme of my childhood was my father returning from a walk upset and angry that yet another hedge had been removed. Mum exhorting him to calm down for the sake of his blood pressure. Having been born in 1919 and always living in the village he had seen immense changes in farming and the land in his life-time. Recording the flora and fauna must also have highlighted the deterioration in the land. In my own childhood stubble was burnt soon after harvest resulting in dark, smoke-filled skies. Crops were heavily sprayed and as teenagers we would hold our breath and run past the sprayer to continue our walks. It was good to see the change in farming now allowing hedges to grow and leaving generous field margins for wildlife and walkers.

I had arranged to have lunch with Dianne who at one point was our neighbour and now lives in another house in Pirton. First I walked past the 1890's yellow Bedfordshire brick terrace house which was my home and where my father had always lived. It is a tiny 'two-up, two-down' house in a row of six houses overlooking a small village green and the village pond. The garden was accessed via a communal backyard. My father bought it off his landlord in the 1950's for £3,000, now it is worth over £200,000!

Dianne treated me to lunch at the 'chapel café' which is in the Methodist church. It is still functioning as a chapel just becoming a café two days a week. A good use of a building. We walked past my old school to the church and looked at my parents' grave. The church is Norman, built from local flint stones and chalk. It is very light and simple inside, the kneelers are embroidered by the parishioners.

Dianne embroidered one in memory of my parents, it is of a purple pasque flower. They are rare orchids which grow on the chalk downland of the nature reserve near the village.

I could have stayed the night but I didn't want to linger long, I always find it hard returning to Pirton now everyone I knew is in the churchyard. There are too many memories and a part of me wants the village to be preserved in a 1960's time-warp with everyone I knew still there. My father's family I can trace back to the 1830's with my great, great grandfather John Burton. I returned alone to the churchyard to pay my respects to my ancestors and say farewell to all the familiar names of people I remember on the gravestones. Then I turned my back on the village and headed up the lane to the hills.

The Icknield Way passes through Pirton. As a child I had been told that it leads to all ways and the rest of the world. Robert Macfarlane in 'Old Ways' reiterates this idea too which I find reassuring as the official Icknield Way is only 170 miles long. It does though lead west to the ancient Ridgeway route and east to the Peddars' Way and the sea at Norfolk. The Icknield Way passes through the village to go up onto the hills along a wide lane known as wood lane. We walked that way every Sunday afternoon. It was encouraging to see how the hedges have been allowed to grow wide and tall and it was peaceful in the late afternoon sunshine. Bare chalk fields showed white leading up to the private woods of the Highdown estate. Dad had been allowed to go into these woods and I had sometimes accompanied him. He would take me to see the keeper's gibbet, a grisly affair of dead animals displayed on a fence which appealed to my curiosity as a child. I treasured those walks with just myself and dad.

There is an old chalk pit where the flints and chalk had been dug out to rebuild the church tower when it collapsed sometime in the early twentieth century. There was a black and white photo in the church vestry of the choir standing amongst the rubble of the tower so as a child I thought the tower had collapsed around them! A massive beech tree stands at the entrance to the chalk pit. Mrs Doarkes, our elderly neighbour had promised to take me and my friends on a picnic there. Sadly she had died during the 1968 flu epidemic, I still recall the sense of being let down on her promise when mum discovered her dead. As a five year old I couldn't grasp the reality of death yet, I was also to lose a favourite great aunt in the same epidemic.

Dad would take me on to Knocking Hoe nature reserve to see the dew pond hidden amongst hawthorn bushes. No streams feed the pond, it is solely formed by rain collecting in a hollow on the hillside. On Good Fridays we would meet the Letchworth naturalists there to see the pasque flowers. Legend has it that they only flower where the blood of Danes fell. Nearby is an ancient burial tumulus, Knocking Hoe, hence the name of the reserve. There was always a 'keep out' sign on the nature reserve gate, now the sign welcomes visitors to the site – the change in attitudes to reserves. Herdwick sheep are being used to keep the downland grass short and prevent hawthorn bushes taking over.

Beyond the nature reserve I walked through a thick carpet of orange beech leaves to the main road. A private sign still remains on a beech tree at the edge of the beech and sycamore wood. There used to be a sign warning 'trespassers will be prosecuted' which had always worried me as I thought it meant persecuted as were the early Christians. Although I knew people were no longer thrown to the lions I was worried what else might happen if you were caught in the woods, although that didn't stop us entering the woods when we got older.

Beyond the main road lies the Deacon Hill, a diminutive

hill of 172metres, it was our nearest hill and the view over Bedfordshire from the top is far reaching. On the first ever May day bank holiday in 1978 my sister, myself and a friend walked up there early to wash our faces in the dew and eat breakfast. There was thick mist as we ate hard boiled eggs sheltering in one of the many hollows on top then blinked in surprise when we climbed out into sunshine. The hollows are relics from neolithic man, it would have been a dry site and easily defended. Some dog walkers and a family with young children, who were rolling down the steep hill, were returning to their cars as I walked up in the setting sun. I wanted to continue to the Pegsdon hills to camp, it is an impressive area of dry chalk valleys which we always knew as 'barn holes' (presumably because you could fit vast barns in the deep valleys). The area is also a nature reserve and there is an information board giving the history of the hills and their usage. I smiled at the drawing of a shepherd for the 1900's as dad began work there as a shepherd age 13 in 1931. He would walk the sheep up to the hills from the village each day and watch them as they grazed, I think he enjoyed it as even as a boy he was interested in wild life.

The wind was getting strong so I hunted around for a flattish, sheltered spot to pitch my tent. It was good to be camping on the open hills for once. The sun set orange and a starry night followed with owls calling and no traffic noise. I awoke to a clear frosty morning and an early morning runner coming past in the semi-darkness. A cockerel was crowing down in Pegsdon village and pheasants were waking up. I packed up early and set out at first light as I had a long day planned walking to Whipsnade and into my mother's past.

The Icknield Way continues as a wide tree-lined track. An orange sunrise accompanied by woodpeckers drumming made it a glorious start to the day. On Sundon Hill the church bells of Harlington were calling the faithful to church. In Sundon village I met a group of litter pickers, the organiser explained they tried to improve the village by clearing up rubbish and planting trees. The year before they had removed seventy cars dumped in a local quarry! I had passed a burnt-out car on the downland but the farmer wouldn't give them permission to tidy it up! It is a hard task as they are near to Luton and further on near the railway line and M1 crossing I came across piles of rubbish as well as the sound of cars racing around. A police car had passed me on a dubious dirt track so I couldn't work out if it was the police car chasing cars or the police themselves driving around fast!

I was heading to Toddington but this involved crossing a field next to an imposing major electrical substation with notices instructing walkers to keep to the designated route to avoid electrocution! It wasn't very scenic although the songs of skylarks accompanied me on the hill up to the village. The shop was a disappointing mix of sweets, pop and alcohol and not much else. A pub was marked on my map at the village of Wingfield, a little further on. It was old and thatched but closed, it evidently hadn't reopened after lockdown. I sat at a picnic bench for lunch. More litter pickers came along, tidying up on a Sunday seemed to be a popular pastime.

The Icknield Way used to go through the outskirts of Luton but the version I was following bypasses the town. However new developments near Houghton Regis meant there were diversions and I ended up off my map. It was only a few miles on a map I had failed to copy but the field was bleak and long and I hoped I was going the right way. Eventually signs led me up to a quiet lane past ancient farmhouses which were no longer farmhouses, just grand houses, until a green lane led me once more onto the downs. A very cheerful young boy, walking with his dad called out a greeting and then I was on the edge of Dunstable. My mother had moved to Dunstable with her parents at the start of world-war two as the book binding company her father worked for relocated there. She had always loved the countryside and animals and had been working at a Blue Cross kennels in London. Now as an eighteen-year old she got a job at Whipsnade zoo which must have been very exciting. I have a couple of photos of her in 1941 holding new born, baby brown bear cubs. Another shows her with a cheetah on a lead.

A steep climb took me up onto Dunstable Downs, an open access area. On that windy, sunny Sunday afternoon hundreds of people were taking advantage of the good weather. A cold wind had picked up, folk were well bundled up in coats with hoods firmly pulled up so that I received some odd looks walking up without a coat on, though I was wearing a hat. But I had a heavy pack and was warm from walking whereas most people had come from heated cars. There are fine views over Bedfordshire and the desire to be airborne; below us noisy planes towed gliders up into the thermals to be released to glide like great pterodactyls. Rooks and red kites soared above and among the brightly coloured kites attached to the hands of earthbound folk and from the steep edges hang-gliders ran and jumped off to soar with the birds. It was a marvellous scene of contentment and enjoyment with no shouting or arguments which has stayed in my mind as such a happy place. I also realised mum must have walked these downs on Sunday afternoons with her parents.

Following the edge of the downs to Whipsnade I arrived at the 'tree cathedral'. It is an arboretum with different tree species representing different sections of the 'cathedral'. Planting began in the 1930's to commemorate three men killed in world-war one and it took two men nine years to finish planting. The trees would have been just young trees when mum was here.

In the church I met a lady locking up who let me fill my water bottle. She was also responsible for locking up the 'cathedral', though I think she meant the gate to the car park as you cannot really lock up an open area with no fence and a footpath through it! I camped on the edge of a large meadow overlooking the zoo carpark and watched the sun setting behind some trees, looking as though they were on fire. The nights were already drawing out as two weeks earlier I had to pitch my tent by 4pm but now it was light at nearly 5pm. The wind picked up during the night, roaring in the trees and buffeting the tent.

The next day was the last day of January and the month was going out like a lion with a bitter north-west wind and gusts of 30mph. It was nothing though compared to the winds back home on the island where I learnt there had been 100mph winds. We had lost part of our kitchen roof and a large length of windbreak had been blown down. I felt guilty being away and not able to help, though I couldn't have repaired the roof and the windbreak wouldn't be needed until the spring.

It was a day to walk through my mother's past starting with an old lane past Whipsnade zoo to the village of Studham where I think she lodged. I wondered if mum had come this way to work. I also realised she had been living only a days walk from Pirton where she would spend her married life and last thirty years. As I followed quiet roads and footpaths through the countryside the road signs pointed to names I recognised from her stories; Jockey End, Markyate, Hudnall, Dagnall. My parents had never owned a car and even though it was close to Pirton we never went to this area, mum lost touch with any friends she had there. Once a group of ladies travelled over to visit, out for a

Sunday afternoon drive, on the chance we would be in as we also didn't have a telephone so couldn't be contacted beforehand. Mum entertained them with scones she quickly made for tea.

When mum had to join the services in the war she chose to join the land army and was sent to nearby Home Farm on the Gaddesden estate. To get there I walked past the Golden Parsonage, an historic old manor house, where as a child I had sat on a rocking horse in the window. My god-mother, auntie Peggy worked there and so had taken me to visit. She had worked for the Halseys, who own the estate, as a house keeper and had lived in a small house on the estate with her father, who had been a gardener. My mother had first met auntie Peggy when she was sent to lodge with her as a twenty-year old when she joined the land army. My mother had been very apprehensive as to what her land lady Miss Wright would be like, it turned out she was only a couple of years older than herself and they became great friends, hence she was our god-mother.

I walked over fields to the black, wooden clad house in Briden's camp where auntie Peggy had lived. It was far smaller than I remembered and I was sad to see the garden overgrown where once there had been colourful flower beds. When my mother first met auntie Peggy she was on her knees weeding, wearing a large sunhat. We used to go and stay there with my mother and I had loved the trees surrounding the house and lying in bed listening to the wood pigeons calling or perhaps it was collared doves who you no longer hear. As teenagers we had cycled over from Pirton to stay the night there, getting lost the first time by Luton airport and sheltering in a church porch during a violent thunder storm.

When auntie Peggy got older and could no longer manage the house the Halseys moved her to a small cottage in the nearby village of Great Gaddesden. The paths there took me past Home Farm where mum had worked in the land army and then Gaddesden Place. The parkland once more ploughed up, this time not for the war effort but by the horses kept there now. We had once gone into the big house when the Halsey's were busy sorting out things for a jumble sale. It was later sold and is now used as the headquarters of Xara Ltd, software developers, as well as being a private house and appearing in films. These old massive estate houses are obviously a huge burden to maintain and must be a daunting legacy. Perhaps that is why the heir chose to become a monk!

Entering Great Gaddesden I detoured to the garden centre and headed for the café as I had been feeling hungry all day. I bought two sausages in a sandwich. I was sticking to a £10/day budget for food, any detour transport and accommodation so couldn't afford the full breakfast which did sound good. Workmen were coming in for their big breakfasts. The old half-timbered house, the middle of three houses, where auntie Peggy had ended up living was nearby. It is a tiny place with very low doorways, I had to duck to enter. As teenagers we would cycle over on a Sunday to visit auntie Peggy bringing some food to cook for dinner and staying until late afternoon, then cycling the three hours back home again. Eventually ill-health meant she moved to a residential home in the early 1990's. I remember visiting with my eldest daughter but as auntie Peggy could barely write it was hard to keep in touch and I never knew when she died.

As I walked up the hill out of the village I thought about my mother and how little I actually knew about her life; my parents married in 1959 and she moved into dad's house in Pirton and made that her life for the next thirty years. I know she was content in the village but it was sad to think she was living so close to old friends but without a car was unable to visit them easily. Visiting auntie Peggy had involved at least three buses and I am not sure if mum was ever able to visit her in later years, she had just heard about her from our visits. Now walking through the countryside I realised how contained we had been living in Pirton, we had always gone on holiday and managed trips to London but been unable to travel in the local area beyond convenient bus routes. Mum had not the energy or time to cycle or walk this far.

Chapter 6

Great Gaddesden to Forest of Dean -old ways and birds

1st-6th Feb

Reunited with the Hertfordshire Way on the hill out of Great Gaddesden I came across an orange robed monk in a yellow waterproof! I was surprised to discover the Amaravati Bhuddist monastery, not what you expect to find in rural Hertfordshire. It was established on the site of an old school. It is possible to visit the monastery but a notice announced that due to covid only pre-booked visits were possible. This was a shame as it would have been interesting to visit a Bhuddist monastery. The place is obviously thriving with new buildings under construction.

The Hertfordshire Way then leads to the Ashridge estate where the lack of signs and the number of paths in the woodland meant I was uncertain which way to go to reach the nearby village of Aldbury. Near the college buildings I approached three middle-aged walkers and asked if they could direct me

"Aldbury is an awfully long way" replied the lady instantly.

"You could go to the café here and use the toilets"

I couldn't be bothered to explain that I was on a long walk and did indeed want to go to Aldbury which turned out to not be far, a forty-five minute walk mostly downhill. The route took me past a prominent monument "in honour of Francis third Duke of Bridgewater father of inland navigation 1832" which seemed appropriate on my walk. I wasn't sure though about the large green urn on top of the monument which looked like it could contain someone's ashes, perhaps it does. There were quite a number of people in the vicinity as there is a small café and gift shop there. It was a good place to stop and sit in the weak sun and eat.

Aldbury is a quintessential English village, nestled below the Chiltern Hills. There is a shop, small school, Norman church and old flint faced cottages scattered around the village green and duck pond complete with the old stocks and whipping post. It's questionable though why somewhere proudly preserves these relics of torture so that they become something scenic to admire and photograph. Aldbury is quiet and feels tucked away, the perfect village. The village shop was also well-stocked so I felt happy as I set off along the road past Tring station with a good supply of food.

I was heading for the Ridgeway long distance path which I could have joined direct from the Icknield Way if I had not made diversions. Two men were replacing a house roof so I was able to fill my water bottle up at an outside tap. My pack was heavy and I was feeling tired so even though it was only 3pm I started to look for somewhere to camp. Finding a quiet corner of a stubble field I pitched my tent by the shelter of a hawthorn hedge. It seemed a good spot to pitch early and rest. I fell asleep. A couple of hours later a tractor drove into the field so I quickly jumped up and went over to the farmer to apologise, expecting him to be cross.

In fact he was quite happy with me camping there but had just come to warn me that the sprayers would be arriving later!

"Will it hurt me?" I asked

"No, they can go round you and it's only glyphosate" he replied "you can stay here if you like but it may be midnight by the time they get here"!

I thanked him for the warning, packed up and left imagining what might have happened had he not come along. I had visions of waking up in the night with my tent dissolving or being squashed flat by a tractor! I resolved to not pitch my tent in rough fields again as I had also presumed no one would work after dark but of course farm machinery has lights. A little further along I found a quiet meadow and put my tent up near an old badgers' sett being careful to avoid obstructing their routes. I didn't want to have animals running into the tent either.

The next few days I headed due west through Buckinghamshire and Oxfordshire to the Forest of Dean where we had lived from 1998 to 2018. Initially following the Ridgeway up and down through beech woods or over downland. I walked through quite a few nature reserves though the approach to managing them is controversial; Combe Hill downland has large areas of eroded chalk where the scrub has been cleared to maintain the grassland. But grass downland isn't natural being the result of man's actions and naturally hawthorn scrub will recolonise the hills. The woodlands also need large old trees to be felled to make light and space for new trees to grow. The countryside we see in Britain has been altered by man throughout history and so none of what is there is really natural.

Descending yet another hill to reach Wendover I felt the Ridgeway was rather a misnomer, I had been climbing and descending hills the entire time, not walking along a ridge.

It was gone 9am as I passed the entrance to the secondary school, a teacher with a clip board was there to reprimand the pupils who were arriving late! Spotting a sign for a bakers I headed that way but all I could see in the window were bars of chocolate! The nearby supermarket was well stocked. Ascending back onto the hills out of Wendover, crossing the railway line and a main road via bridges I was puzzled to pass boarded up houses. The first were old terrace houses, I presumed they were unsafe but then I passed big detached houses with no entry signs. It was strange until the sign "HS2 a bridge too far for Wendover" revealed the reason. Higher up I could see the linear scar of the high speed railway construction approaching the edge of Wendover where there will be a high fly-over. I thought of all the people forcibly moved from their homes along the length of the railway route and the parallel this lowland clearance has with the Highland clearances of the past. It has happened throughout history, people forced off their land and from their homes to make way for canals then railways then motorways (or sheep in the case of the Highlands). It is not something we think about as we drive around the country but seeing the reality was a shock. I also feel sorry for the people whose houses are not in the way but will now be living right beside the new railway line cut off from Wendover by yet another obstruction.

A few miles further on in grass parkland I followed a line of notices on posts regarding trespassing;

"this is a protected site under section 128 of the serious organised crime and police act 2005. Trespass on this site is a criminal offence."

There was no fence, just the regularly spaced posts. Some distance to the right I could see a large country house. How strange I thought, the owners of the house must be paranoid about trespassers. Coming to the driveway with locked gates, security cameras and more notices it all became clear. I was walking by Chequers! It is a quiet, secluded location out of sight of the HS2 route. The extensive grounds would be ideal to build a new community in which to house the displaced people, they would probably be happy. As I climbed the next hill beside more warning notices I wondered what would happen if you were to stray beyond the signs. My son suggested I should have run across the grassland naked as streakers get a lesser sentence due to mental instability! Great! I suppose at least the Ridgeway path is permitted to go through the edge of the grounds.

At Princes Risborough I bought a pie and chips, the last cooked dinner I had eaten was ten days ago at Anna's. I felt empty. Sitting in the churchyard to eat I was joined on my seat in the sun by a sprightly 86 year old. She had moved there the year before to be near her daughter, sadly her husband had since died, they had been married for 65 years! To keep herself going she goes for a daily walk though due to her age has to sit down for rests. She set off again at a good pace.

The constant ups and downs of the Ridgeway had been tiring, I was not looking forward to the Oxfordshire Way which I was going to follow for the next few days. Maps can be deceptive, I anticipated difficult to follow footpaths through uninspiring countryside with noisy main roads. How wrong I was. The Oxfordshire Way turned out to be one of the most relaxing sections of my walk. I was on the longest uninterrupted part of my walk so far and fell in to a non-pressured routine. I had five days to reach a friend near Cheltenham. All that was required of me was to eat, walk, sleep, repeat. To quote Bill Bryson

"time ceases to have any meaning. When it is dark you go to bed and when it is light again you get up, and everything in between is just in between. It's quite wonderful really."

Phoning a daughter she said I was the most chilled out ever and should just keep walking! I began to see why there were tramps in the past, often men who did have money but who had chosen an itinerant life.

Following old ways I passed through quiet villages, some with thatched cottages, surrounded by old meadows. I walked west into the setting sun, camping on the edge of fields each night and following well signed routes each day. The first snowdrops were appearing and I came across some lambs in a sheltered meadow. Near the surprisingly quiet M40 I saw fleeing roe deer and so many birds. Woodpeckers are the birds I associate with this area, it wasn't unusual to hear several drumming from different directions. A green woodpecker almost tripped me up as it shot out of a hedge. A sparrow hawk had exited the same hedge and it also held a flock of small finches including, I think, yellowhammers, though they never stayed still long enough for me to be certain. People were also few and far between and I would walk for hours seeing no one.

Sydenham is mentioned in the Doomsday book and is an idyllic village of old brick houses, some thatched and converted old black barns surrounded by overgrown meadows. On the village green the large wooden bus shelter is also a 'book swap' and the old red telephone kiosk houses the defibrillator. Further on someone had been rather enthusiastic creosoting the wooden barns and gates so that some came off on my hands.

I passed through the ancient villages of Rycote and Tiddington to Waterstock. They are very peaceful despite being near to Oxford but under threat as developers want to turn the neighbouring golf course into a 500 acre industrial hub, it is by the M40/A40 junction. At times it felt like the countryside was at threat of being completely covered with tarmac and buildings. At Waterperry I discovered a fascinating free rural museum. Entering I found myself in a barnlike room absolutely packed with old rural paraphernalia. It is the retirement collection of Gordon Dempster who chats eagerly to visitors and is full of historical knowledge. My eye was attracted to a useful spade, the 'gamekeeper's friend'; the head being a spade, axe and measure and the handle serving as a hammer and an awl. In a display case were a pair of 1937 Dunlop rubber sheep boots designed to prevent sheep rot! I think they would only have been used on prize sheep as they would not have been very cheap and with the coming of the war they were discontinued. I bought a postcard of them to send to my eldest daughter as she keeps sheep. It would take hours to study all the exhibits but I wanted to press on.

At Beckley, a small village of pale Cotswold stone houses, the children were walking down to the small school past the snowdrop covered churchyard. A notice announced that mole traps had been set, marked by canes. I wasn't sure whether moles shouldn't perhaps be allowed to live in churchyards. The rhyme the man in the museum recited kept repeating itself in my head;

"I went to Noke but no one spoke
I went to Thame it was just the same
Burford, Brill were silent and still
But I went to Beckley and they spoke directly"

He said it dated back to the riots which I think were in 1829 when the peasants rose up against the draining and fencing off of the Ot moor area of marshland which would deprive them of common grazing. The other places mentioned are all in the same vicinity and so were visited in an attempt to catch the culprits. The Ot moor is fenced off and forms an extensive wetland area, presumably full of wildlife.

Nearer Oxford I left the Oxfordshire Way as it takes a circuitous route and joined the Oxford Greenbelt Way which was noisier being nearer main roads and the railway line, but still very rural. On a bridge crossing the A34 dual carriageway was a lady in her 60's taking photos and waving to lorry drivers. When a lorry driver hooted her face broke into an ecstatic smile. I pondered about the pleasure she obviously got, she was one of the happiest people I saw and probably cheered up the lorry drivers too. She was certainly happier than the dog walkers I passed in that area who deliberately avoided eye contact and saying hello. I am afraid to say they were the most anti-social people I met on my entire walk.

Gosford on the edge of Oxford was depressing with rubbish strewn along the paths and dumped behind houses, yet adjacent Kidlington has large Cotswold stone houses and no rubbish. At Thrupp I joined the Oxford canal which was very tranquil with well-maintained barges and neat gardens on the banks, a contrast to the Lea valley canal. I had a strange encounter at Shipton with a very flustered, red-faced man in a baggy pin-striped suit and multi-patterned canvas shoes. He had already stopped two cars to ask for directions but with no help so I called to him that I had a map. Commenting that he seemed very stressed he said he was late for an appointment, needing to get to Shipton quarry. On my map I could see what was possibly a quarry nearby so directed him there. He sped off leaving me wondering whether he was late to dispose of a body or some such dubious appointment......it was his unusual attire and his level of agitation which confused me, also most people have access to a phone and directions. I decided I had been walking too long by myself allowing my imagination to run riot though I did check up later as to whether there is a functioning quarry at Shipton. There is, so perhaps no body was involved.

I entered the Cotswolds at the attractive town of Woodstock feeling tired and hungry. Whenever I felt weary my pack always felt heavier and seemed to rub my hips. I went shopping then sat by the Queen's pool in Blenheim palace grounds to eat, it wasn't very attractive as the edges were being cleared ready for dredging in the spring. The palace is rather a monstrosity of a building. There is a very tall monument to victory in the grounds but I didn't walk that way so I am not sure which victory. On the Ridgeway I had passed a tall monument to those who died in South Africa 1899-1902, the victory of the Boer war. I do not like these monuments, Britain's victory was someone else's defeat.

One morning it snowed as I packed up my tent from the corner of a field. The flakes coming down were like petals and for some reason the 'Floral Dance' kept running through my head. The snow soon stopped and the day remained dry but overcast.

Enroute to Chipping Norton I joined the Wychwood Way which follows the Salt Path. A board informed me that this was an Anglo-Saxon route along which salt had been transported from Droitwich to Princes Risborough for distribution. Later the route was used for driving cattle to market. I wish I was more familiar with ancient history and am amazed at how many ancient ways still remain in England and have escaped tarmac or development. I also did not know about the salt trade in the area and realised how much about Britain I was learning on this walk.

In the Glyme valley before Chipping Norton there is a lovely clear stream running through a meadow where I thought I might camp in readiness for the parkrun the next day. It was too early to set up camp though so I went into Chipping Norton first and to the library. I wanted to catch up on emails and to check up on parkrun too, which was as well as I discovered that it had not restarted yet since covid. I decided to keep walking, but first visited the shops and came across a proper bakers crammed full of wonderful goodies. Bakers had been very scarce so far and I am a great lover of cake. I opted for rolls and an impressive hunk of bread pudding.

It was disappointing about the parkrun but I blamed myself for not researching fully before starting my walk. It did mean though I could get ahead of my scheduled mileage and press on westwards. The Cotswolds were harder to find camp spots in though as the fields were either full of horses or ploughed with no wide margins or had 'private' signs. At dusk I ended up camping on some rough ground by a village in plain view of half a dozen houses, if anyone had cared to look out of their bedroom windows. It was a clear night with a crescent moon and there was a hard frost in the morning.

The next day I entered Gloucestershire at Bledington where outside the well-stocked community shop were posters advertising a marmalade competition. The marmalades would be judged on texture, taste and flavour but no jars would be returned. This conjured up images of some marmalade loving person being the judge in order to gain a years supply of marmalade, albeit with the jars opened and sampled. It was all very much WI 'Jam and Jerusalem' England but it made me smile.

The Oxfordshire Way continues into Gloucestershire, finishing at Bourton-on-the-water (making it a bit of a misnomer). Entering estate land I struggled in the mud on the bridleway so switched to an easier to walk track running parallel. I stepped to the side as an off-road vehicle approached, it slowed down;

"Can you stay on the footpath, on the bridleway over there" said a rather well-spoken man.

I explained that the bridleway was rather muddy and slippery being cut up by horses, almost adding that I wasn't a horse.

"In future walk on it" he replied.

Continuing in a patronising tone he asked where I was going with my pack. A notice had stated that the estate was farmed for wildlife and requested that dogs be kept on leads to not disturb wildlife. I rather felt that the vehicle was disturbing wildlife more than myself, I felt annoyed. It was the first and only time that anyone 'told me off' on my walk.

Another first and only occurrence happened following on from that incident when I got lost and ended up in a village a couple of miles away from where I thought I was. The section of map I was using was rather out of date and the Oxfordshire Way wasn't very clearly marked so I had got confused and on reaching a church thought I was somewhere else. It is surprising how similar two old villages with a few houses and a church can appear on a map!

The third incident that day was slipping over, again the only time it ever happened. It was very muddy approaching Bourton-on-the-water and I ended up sitting on my bottom. I was unhurt but in a puzzle how to get up again with a heavy pack on and my feet slithering on the mud. Entering the village I hoped I didn't look too dirty though I probably looked out of place amongst the well-dressed day trippers enjoying the sun and the stream. It was a bit of a shock seeing so many people having walked through so many empty Cotswold villages. Even on a Saturday I had heard no sound of children. Most of the villages are made up of large houses built from pale Cotswold stone with stone window surrounds and I presume lots of planning restrictions about what colour paint you can use and what you can do. They are attractive villages but I found them rather austere and soul less being so preserved with no variations.

I wanted to sit down for lunch and there round the corner was the 'Shalom Rainbow café' where you pay a donation, a welcome place for a long lunch break. At another table sat half a dozen locals who could have been the cast for a cross between 'The vicar of Dibley' and 'Last of the summer wine'. It made an entertaining lunch listening to discussions on catching rabbits, corporal punishments when they were at school, Boris Johnson and as to whether one of their number was wearing socks! I left Bourton and picked up the Windrush Way which goes to Winchcombe, though only following the actual Windrush valley at times. The river was narrow but deep and very clear, tempting for a swim if it had been warmer. There were carpets of snowdrops. A group of young men came towards me discussing which pub they hoped to get to. The route was very muddy and the wind picked up. I struggled to find somewhere to camp, ending up in a hollow in a meadow, hoping no land owner would tell me to move.

The next day I reached Winchcombe and walked briefly with a couple walking part of the Cotswold Way. I was heading to Cleeve common where lots of people were enjoying the windy, sunny Sunday morning. It was amusing when two dog owners almost went off with the wrong dog – identical chestnut Labradors both with red collars!

I stopped at Cleeve Hill trig point to take in the views; behind me was southern England and in front was the West and Wales. I had completed the southern section of my walk, next was the Welsh borders. I had walked almost 300 miles, it felt good, though I still had a long way to go. A couple with a dog kindly took a photo so for once I had legs too rather than just a head when taking 'selfies'. They were pleased I could reciprocate so there was both of them plus dog in a photo. A party of about eighteen walkers were sheltering in a hollow to eat lunch, the wind was very strong up by the summit.

Today was only a half day, I descended the hill to catch up with an old friend in Woodmancote. Pam walks long-distance paths and has covered a lot of Britain over the years so we were not lost for things to talk about. She was polite & didn't comment about my unwashed state as we sat & talked for five hours at the lunch table! On getting up I struggled to walk as my feet had become swollen sitting down so long. Camping I always sat down with my feet raised in my tent so never had that problem. Solution was to lie on the floor with my feet in the air after my shower whilst Pam cooked a delicious dinner. It was good too to sleep in a bed after fourteen consecutive days camping out.

We also discussed the strange tale of her neighbour's wife who seemed to have disappeared to Sri Lanka! The neighbour told her that his wife was helping in a children's home there but Pam thought that she had probably left him and he was trying to save face. It all sounded rather strange but I had also had a strange conversation with my eldest daughter a few days earlier. She had rung me upset that an old man who had 'adopted' her and my grand-daughter had died. The next day though his daughter rang her and asked if she had had a good Christmas. Apparently he had told her that he had spent Christmas on the Isle of Lewis and had fabricated a long story about buying a house and sheep in the village. She had even been shown photos of the place and the sheep, which were infact photos of my daughter's sheep! The man had been delusional and created the dream life he had wanted. A curious situation but perhaps something you cannot blame someone for, we all have our dreams. I jokingly had assured my daughter that I was indeed fulfilling my dream and wasn't just pretending to walk the length of the country.

Chapter 7

Forest of Dean; friends and river Wye

7th-12th Feb

It was the end of week four, time for a rest. I had planned to spend the week in the Forest of Dean with friends. We had lived there for almost twenty years after moving there in 1998, a few months before my son was born until we moved to the Isle of Lewis at the end of 2017. Initially we had lived on a housing estate in the large village of Bream on the south side of the forest before moving to the former mining village of Lydbrook, on the other side of the forest by the river Wye.

The Forest of Dean is not a particularly large area being just over 526 square kilometres but it is a very distinct district with an identity separate from Gloucestershire, which it is part of. The towns and villages are mostly round the edges with the rivers Wye and Severn forming boundaries to the west and south. When living there it seems a long way across the forest, all the trees forming a psychological as well as a physical barrier.

My first stop was to visit my friends Dave and Gaynor

who live in Longhope on the Gloucester side of the forest. I planned to catch a train and then bus there, partly because the footpaths between Cheltenham and Gloucester are not very scenic but also because I wanted to arrive there in time for lunch. This meant I could meet other friends who come to Gaynor's on a Monday to weave. I did however walk from Pam's to Cheltenham where I followed the Honeybourne way to Cheltenham spa station. It was a great disappointment as 'honey' is too sweet a name for a route starting at an ugly electricity substation and competing with London for graffiti. It definitely gives a different view of Cheltenham from the elegant former spa town with its pleasant shops, grand town hall and genteel gardens. Although the route was busy barely anyone spoke or said hello.

It was a relief to reach the station and catch a train to Gloucester and then the bus to Longhope. I have known Gaynor and Dave for about fourteen years and have spent many happy hours at their place weaving and in the garden helping Gaynor. It was a relaxing place to spend a few days. I was also able to catch up with two more friends who come to weave, Liz and Suzanne. I first met Liz nearly sixteen years ago and am impressed at how busy and active she still is at 84 years young. Gaynor was recovering from major spinal surgery and it was good to find her more mobile than I had feared.

Lunch was lovely; good wholesome, home-made food, a welcome change from the packaged food I had to resort to camping. I also hoped the days off and the good food would help me regain the couple of pounds I had lost on the walk. My heels were sore and blistered so some non-walking days would hopefully help them. I was annoyed with myself that they had been rubbed but it was a combination of the mileage and experimenting with thinner socks and different insoles.

There was still one trip into my childhood to make which involved a pleasant half-day walk from their house. My surrogate auntie Winnie and uncle Phil had lived in the nearby village of Clifford's Mesne and I had spent many happy summer days at their house. My father had met uncle Phil during the war when they were both posted on the search-lights. It was a life-long friendship. When I was two and a half they had driven over to Pirton with their two youngest children, Margaret and Morris (who were about ten years older than Sarah) for a surprise visit. We hadn't got a phone so they couldn't warn us and mum had never met them. She and auntie Winnie became firm friends and mum would stay there with us, we would share a double bed with mum in the middle.

Auntie Winnie and uncle Phil lived in an old house below May Hill surrounded by meadows and trees with a large productive garden. The forest supplied all their wood for cooking and heating. Their son Morris had worked in the forest with the last working horse there, Norman, a large grey gentle beast. In the meadow in front of the house they kept hens and a milking cow.

Dave led the way through the extensive network of footpaths to the summit of May Hill. Trotting along behind I enjoyed the luxury of walking unburdened without a pack and glad to have a guide to save route finding. May Hill is a prominent landmark for miles around with its groups of fir trees on top. I had seen it from Cleeve Hill already. Uncle Phil used to drive up in his old post office van as auntie Winnie was severely disabled with arthritis. The view from the top is extensive over to the Cotswolds and Malvern Hills across Herefordshire to the Black Mountains and the Brecon Beacons in Wales and then the Severn estuary with Somerset beyond. To me, as a child, it was the most amazing view and the highest place I ever went to.

When the Black Mountains were pointed out I thought it was a foreign country. Coming from Hertfordshire it might as well have been a foreign country, the landscape was so different and the people's accents so strange. The summit of May Hill is also where many people's ashes are scattered, including auntie Winnie's and uncle Phil's.

The Forest of Dean and May Hill are 'right to roam' areas too, it was nice to be back somewhere where you can walk at will and not be restricted to a few paths. We dropped down through the forest to the edge of Clifford's Mesne where there are numerous narrow green lanes. I led the way hoping to find the right way to Rose cottage and there it was. It was good to see the old house again, little changed and the back garden still used for growing vegetables. The meadow in front was smaller than I remembered but it was still quiet and peaceful, surrounded by forest.

A couple of days later, refreshed, well fed and with clean clothes I said good bye and headed off through the forest to Lydbrook. Dave had volunteered to drive me over to Bream to see our old house there but I had no great desire to visit it. It had been a small modern house on a large housing estate and it seemed a waste of time and fuel to drive so far. I had never walked the initial route to Lydbrook before so it felt good to explore a different area of the forest.

At Brierley I followed the fence of the beaver enclosure and could just make out their dam down below in the trees. It felt slightly like a zoo as the beavers are fenced in an area. They were introduced shortly before we moved with the idea to stop flooding on the Great Hough Brook which runs down through Lydbrook. I am not sure what happens if they rear young and where they will go, the enclosure isn't that extensive. (I later learnt that the female died and the male did not get a companion for a couple of years). It would be great if beavers could wander where they will but then there is the issue of roads and dogs and whether the beavers would build dams where it is convenient for people. In other areas of the country where beavers have been introduced, such as Aberdeenshire there are major conflicts with the farmers.

We had lived for almost sixteen years in Lydbrook, an old coal and tin mining village squeezed in a long dark valley running down from the edge of the forest to the river Wye. We had lived in three different houses in the village gradually moving down the valley, ending up by the river Wye. Our first house was a former vicarage beside the forest and church. The children spent many happy hours balancing on the churchyard wall (and occasionally falling off) and swinging on a rope hung over a sycamore branch. The trees have now been cut down and a fence erected inside the wall so it looked less exciting for the current young occupants. Following the line of the old railway down the valley I had glimpses of the houses huddled along the road. It appeared less gloomy than I remembered as more houses seemed to be painted cheerful colours, a good idea when the sun does not reach the valley for three months of the winter.

For almost ten years we had rented an old brick and stone cottage in Lower Lydbrook. It had been falling down and was cold and damp but it had a good garden and was in a nice location. The children had been able to roam freely in the area, climbing the remains of the old viaduct and in the summer swimming in the river. When we moved out the landlord had replaced the ancient draughty sash windows and renovated the house, it has since sold and looked quite presentable. The garden had been productive with cordon apple trees, strawberries, raspberries, herbs and vegetables, it is now mostly grass and seemed so much smaller. The children had played hide and seek with friends, crouching down among the raspberries or behind the runner beans or dropping down into the stream which ran beside the garden.

I sat for a while overlooking the river where there is a grassy bank and innumerable memorial seats. At some point the seats were becoming too plentiful so no more are allowed, instead people can commission brass plaques which line the handrail of a footbridge over the stream. A lady in a nearby house came over and greeted me as if I had never been away. I looked at the time, nearly 12.30pm, I had a lunch appointment with a previous neighbour John, which was delicious and good to catch up with an old friend.

Our last few years in the forest were spent in another falling down rented house overlooking the river Wye. It had a marvellously big garden where we had had free roaming hens and ducks and views over the river to woodland where we would watch deer. It had though been a north facing site so for several months in the winter caught no sun and when it froze we would remain white when everywhere else was green. I knocked on the door of the old neighbours, John and Daphne but they were out so I ended up catching up with them the next day.

It was past 3pm when I left the village, which was by then in deep shadow and cold but as I climbed up through the sheep fields to the nearby village of English Bicknor I re-emerged into warm sunshine and daylight. I realised I did not miss the cold and gloom of Lydbrook. I had been invited to dinner with friends Eric and Gillian and the offer of 'glamping' in their summer house. I didn't stay in the house as they were still worried about covid, due to health issues. I ate meals at the other end of their table with the window open! It was a cold, frosty night with a bright moon so I was glad of the cup of tea in the morning brought by Gillian, I joked that it was the first on the trip, no one had appeared at my tent with one!

I had another offer of a bed that night in the village at Jane and Dave's and Jane could also drop me in Monmouth that day so I could walk back to the forest. I ended up walking the ten miles along the river between Monmouth and the forest in the opposite direction to the rest of my walk! It was useful being in Monmouth as I needed to shop for a few things, it is also a town I am very familiar with as three of my children attended secondary school there. Sadly there were quite a number of empty shops at the top of the High Street and an application for an amusement arcade where a music shop had been.

The next day Jane kindly dropped me off for the Forest of Dean parkrun where it was good to meet some familiar faces. Parkrun here was the reason I began running about ten years ago and it was good to run the old route. It is quite challenging as it twists and turns on narrow paths amongst the trees. Tea and coffee afterwards had restarted since covid and gave me a chance to catch up with folk. I needed though to meet Pam in Monmouth at 10.30 as she was joining me for a nineteen-mile day and so was grateful for the lift there with a fellow parkrunner.

Meeting Pam by the bus station we headed off along the Offa's Dyke path out into the Monmouthshire countryside. Years previously my children and I had walked parts of the Offa's Dyke path on day trips colouring in sections on a rough map of the route. I had never walked the section out of Monmouth and was pleasantly surprised at how soon we were out of town and walking through the small fields of Monmouthshire. I was excited to be on the Welsh borders section of my walk though little did I know that it would be the most challenging week of the entire trip. It was pleasant walking that day and good to be in company. I had been a little apprehensive about walking with someone, would we be different speeds? But we settled into a comfortable pace and the miles went past.

It was just after mid-day when we reached the hamlet of Llanvihangel Ystern-Llewern (these wonderful Welsh names) so we sat in the church porch to eat lunch. I was amused by the strategically placed defib there. A couple came along and asked if we wanted to see inside the church and at the mention of a toilet I said yes. The church had recently received a grant for the toilet and in the summer will be unlocked daily so walkers can make use of it and the kettle provided for drinks, an excellent idea. We were encouraged to sign the visitors book so they could show the footfall to help with future grant applications.

At Llanvihangel Crucorney we left the Offa's Dyke path to follow footpaths west to Abergavenny. We were also trying to contact another friend, Morag, who was travelling from Swansea and going to walk out and meet us, slightly tricky when the phone reception was very patchy. It started to rain gently so we donned waterproofs. It was the first rain of my walk! Eventually at 4pm we reached the minor road from Abergavenny where we had arranged to meet Morag and there she was walking towards us. Morag, Pam and I were all at university together, although I had met Morag the summer before, so they are my longest standing friends. Whenever we meet up we comfortably slip into conversation as old friends can, so it was a nice walk mostly downhill into town. Morag had helpfully worked out a route to get us through the town to Llanfoist where we were staying. It was dark and raining harder by the time we arrived at the air bnb but our hosts were unfussed with our wet gear and clothing. Dinner was eaten in the nearby Brewer's Fayre, not out of choice, it was the only place. Pudding was forgone to return to the bnb for hot chocolate and to share a chocolate orange a friend who couldn't make it to parkrun had sent me!

Chapter 8

Welsh Borders; wet and wild

13th-20th Feb

The next day it was raining hard. After an excellent breakfast I set off in the rain along the Brecon canal which hugs the hillside just above Llanfoist. Pam and Morag were offered a lift to the station. I was going to follow the canal to Brecon. It is a beautiful canal and very peaceful. A contrast to how busy and noisy it must have been when it was first constructed. Along the way information boards explain the history of the area and there are benches carved with a map of the canal and a red dot marking where you are, but frustratingly no mileage markers. It was useful to be following a canal as there was no need of a map on such a wet day, I couldn't get lost.

At Llangattock I went into a pub to get out of the rain for a while and dry out. I bought chips and mince to eat. The bartender must have been feeling sorry for me as a little later a man came in asking if they served light lunches and was told they were fully booked up with Sunday dinners. I sat and read a local magazine and the article about a mountain rescue. A man had not returned from a walk up the Skirrid, a small hill near Abergavenny. It had taken over eight hours to find him as he had made a shelter from the rain, it was a bit scary to think how hidden someone could be. It also highlighted the importance of the mountain rescue teams.

The rain eased up a bit as I continued, there was no one around except the occasional dog walker. I was now seeing 'proper' dogs; collies, Labradors and large cross-breeds. In urban areas I had seen lots of miniature dogs and the now very popular French bulldogs. I chatted to a dog walker who had done photography for Green-peace and who knew Stornoway.

The last time I had been along the canal was in 2017, on my bicycle, one late autumn afternoon. The tow path had been busy then with walkers and cyclists and I had to dismount to go under the low bridges. The late sun had glinted through the leaves, it had been a cycle ride I didn't want to end.

Finding a flat area of grass by picnic benches I set up camp with a view of the canal and one of the attractive stone bridges. The rain stopped, birds were singing, it felt good to be in my tent again. The morning dawned dry and still, the trees and bridges perfectly reflected in the dark waters of the canal. I watched a heron and a dipper. It was only a half-day walk to Brecon where I was staying the night with another friend from university, Heather. I had doctored my heels with compeed but they still hurt, the shorter days walk would be good for them. Clouds covered the Black mountains. My original plan had been to walk through them to Brecon via a small bothy by the reservoir at Grynne Fawr. I am very fond of the Black mountains having spent many days walking in them but I was glad to not be up on the hills in the rain and low clouds as there were some heavy showers.

Brecon is the base for a lot of army training and as I

neared the town a chinook helicopter came over almost skimming the treetops. It is ironic or perhaps appropriate that there is a peace garden in Brecon next to the army store. I spent a pleasant afternoon and evening at Heather's cuddling her westie-lapsung cross dog, I was in need of some 'doggy' therapy missing mine.

It was still raining the next day when I went to catch the bus to Hay-on-Wye to re-join the Offa's Dyke path. I was enjoying being back in Wales where everyone is so friendly, the lady in the fruit and veg shop offered to put the fruit into my pack to save me taking it off my back! In the bakers they were worried that I was walking in the rain. I could have spent some time browsing in the numerous bookshops, Hay being a book town, but I wanted to press on it already being 11am. In my diary I wrote that the day was marvellous, the rain stopped after an hour and hazy views of the hills opened up. Birds sang and the banks were white with snowdrops. I saw no one apart from three men fixing electricity cables until I dropped down to Kington. At the tiny village of Newchurch I spied a welcome sign in the churchyard, 'church open, tea, coffee'. The church does not have running water but there were bottles of water, a kettle, tea, coffee, squash, biscuits. Brilliant. Thank you to the kind parishioners of Newchurch, I wish churches in the south could follow this example.

Everywhere was very wet underfoot and where the route went through sheep fields extremely muddy. The sheep are grazed on root crops and I felt sorry for them as they were so wet and muddy. At least it wasn't the tacky mud of Kent but it was very slippery, a sledge would have been useful on downhill sections. I climbed up on to Hergest ridge where the walking was easy and the sheep white and fluffy. There are poems on the marker posts and on the summit a group of monkey puzzle trees! Planted as part of the Hergest estate they are a landmark for miles around. It was a long way downhill to Kington, passing several dog walkers climbing up, I was glad to be going down.

I didn't reach the town until gone 5pm so sadly the small independent shops were closed but I bought food in a small supermarket then went to investigate whether the campsite was open, it wasn't. Retracing my steps back up the hill and finding no suitable fields I went into the churchyard and pitched next to the compost bins in the dusk. A lady with her son in a car said I wouldn't be in the way as it wasn't scouts that night. I thought it would be quiet and out the way but half the residents of Kington seemed to run or walk past with their dogs, including the vicar. He enquired if I was okay and I replied that I was fine but wasn't sure if his bicycle was because at that moment his black Labrador pulled it over and began dragging it away! (the scene made more dramatic by the red lights round the dog's neck). Anyway the vicar was happy with me camping there and went off to the vicarage next door. He could have invited me in for dinner or breakfast or both but I suppose I caught him by surprise. I presume he doesn't come across ladies camping in the churchyard every night.

The next days walk to Knighton was a struggle and turned out to be the hardest day of the week. It was dry to pack up but began to rain soon after setting out. The wind became increasingly strong so I was fighting a side wind and being buffeted about. Martha had warned me that storm Dudley was approaching, the first of a series of storms predicted that week. The Offa's Dyke path climbs up on to exposed hills of 300/400m then twice drops down into big wide valleys. I slithered and slipped, struggling on the wet mud and at one point climbed over a fence to rescue a sheep who had slipped over on to her side. She was hopefully flailing her legs, uselessly turning in semi-circles on the mud, creating 'mud angels'. I heaved her to her feet on the mud and thankfully she trotted off. I felt very weary, my heels hurt with every step and my feet felt leaden. I arrived wet and cold in Knighton at lunchtime so went into the first café I found to revive myself on egg and chips and decide what to do.

Heavy rain was forecast for the afternoon and the next section of the route was high up and exposed with no hope of shelter. I needed to find shelter and stop so I splashed out £30 for a room in the George and Dragon pub which was lovely. I went to ground with a hot shower and a book. It was the lowest point of the walk, I was behind schedule, my feet hurt, storms were threatening and the Offa's Dyke path was far more challenging than I had anticipated. If I was struggling now, how would I manage the Pennine Way? I stayed put on the bed, got lost in a detective book, drank lots of mugs of tea and ate. It was time out I needed, I had been fighting the wind and mud all day and hadn't kept myself hydrated and although it was enjoyable meeting up with friends I needed time to shut down. I re-evaluated my walk; it didn't matter if I didn't stick to my timetable which I had partly devised around parkruns. There were no rules, it was my walk. My next planned parkrun was to be in Oswestry but I realised I would not reach there in time and also my planned route beyond there was via paths beside the river Dee to Chester. This would now be flooded and having omitted to pack an inflatable dingy I must change my route. I was due to spend a couple of days with my in-laws on the Wirral the next week and had planned to catch a train there from Chester but I could instead keep to the west and head to Wrexham. I could also arrive there a few days later if needed. The only deadline I had was to arrive in Sheffield by the Friday as I was meeting my daughter, Martha, there as she was joining me for part of the Pennine Way. If needs be I could catch a train between the Wirral and Sheffield to make up time.

A good rest and night's sleep saw me up and out early in a much better frame of mind. There was a full moon still out and a pink sunrise as I climbed up out of Knighton, passing the Welsh/English border into the Shropshire hills. I followed the bank of the Offa's Dyke all day up and down the hills. It is quite distinct being over ten feet high in places often with trees on top. I could see the line of the dyke snaking over the land climbing in and out of the deep valleys with lots of very steep ascents and descents. The climbs though were short and the going underfoot easy. It was a good day, beautiful countryside with hedges white with snowdrops. I saw few houses and passed no one, Shropshire seemed to be a county of sheep. On an almost vertical climb above Newcastle a sign announces the half-way point on the Offa's Dyke, eighty-eight and a half miles to Prestatyn in the north or the same distance to Chepstow in the south. I couldn't decide whether that would give walkers of the entire route encouragement or not.

I sat in the isolated churchyard of Churchtown for a break surrounded by woods and snowdrops and listening to the plaintive, repetitive voice of woodpigeons. Liz had said it sounded like they were saying "my feet ache Betty", a phrase I couldn't get out of my head and which at times had me telling the birds to stop complaining, especially when my own feet ached!

I made for Montgomery which was a detour off the Offa's Dyke but I had to be inside for the night. Storm Eunice was forecast threatening 90mph winds from early the next morning. I followed the edge of Mellington Hall and its holiday caravans. They did not look very prepared for the storm with garden furniture sitting outside and tall trees beside them. It felt like people in England did not realise the intensity of such strong winds; my father-in-law had agreed it could be dangerous walking with trees falling down but I had pointed out that in winds above 40mph it was impossible to walk without being blown over myself! I caught up with a lady resting on a fallen tree trunk, the first walker I had met all day. She was being met at the road by her husband (who I had already met by the church at Churchtown) and they were staying in the Dragon Hotel in Montgomery.

Arriving in Montgomery I called in at the Dragon Hotel where I had stayed almost eight years ago with my eldest daughter for her twenty first birthday. Then it had been a slightly rundown but cosy pub, it is now a smart hotel and the best they could do was £89 for B&B, rather beyond my budget. It does include breakfast they had assured me, I hoped so. The couple I had met were obviously better off than me! There was no answer at the nearby B&B, the only other accommodation in Montgomery so I went to investigate the church porch. It is very large and would have been dry, albeit draughty but then Denise at the post office rang around and I found myself at Helen and Steve's for the night with a comfy bed, shower and breakfast. Helen is a walker so we chatted about walks, she recounted how a man living nearby beside the Offa's Dyke path had walked round Wales. He had simply turned right out of his front door, following the Offa's Dyke path south to the coast, round the Welsh coast to return back down the Offa's Dyke to his house. He had planned the walk but it did make me think it was a spontaneous walk having just gone out for a while, as in 'The unlikely pilgrimage of Harold Fry'. That is a thought provoking, fictitious tale of a man walking the length of Britain having just gone out to post a letter.

In the morning it turned out the storm had largely missed Shropshire causing much damage further south, newspaper front pages had photos of the damaged O2 building in London. There were also warnings of further storms, the tabloids having illustrations of Frankenstein and his friends to come (the next storm on the way being storm Franklin). I was able to carry on walking but decided to stay low down and also needed to be able to cross the flooded River Severn. Helen suggested I headed along the canal to Welshpool and explained which route to take over the river to avoid the floods. I was walking off my map again but the directions to the canal were clear and simple, mainly along quiet roads. Approaching a steep hill I saw an elderly lady walking down towards me only to reach the bottom of the hill and 'rewind' by walking backwards up the hill! She said it was easier and strengthened her thigh muscles.

The Montgomery canal is partly silted up and covered with reeds, it creates a linear wild-life reserve. It began to rain and I could hear the wind roaring in the trees on the hills, I was glad I had stayed low down. I chatted to a lady who had moved down from a high-up hill farm where they had had cattle and sheep. She looked in her sixties and had recently left her husband, I didn't like to ask why. She was a long-distance lorry driver so interested in my walk. I half hoped she would invite me back for a coffee but I had already passed her canal-side house. Underneath a bridge gave escape from the rain for a break.

Welshpool is an earthy, lived-in town. I was wet so popped into the library by the canal which also has a museum upstairs. I used the computer then went in search of a second-hand bookshop where I managed to buy a map for my route to Wrexham for only £2. Passing a sign for a physiotherapist and chiropractor I was tempted to call in but then they may recommend not walking daily with a large rucksack. I had also on my travels walked past chiropodist signs but thought they might be horrified at the state of my feet. I decided that any 'treatment' would probably be best left until I had finished walking and would not undo any good work some therapy might achieve.

I followed the canal out of town, it runs parallel to the A483 beyond which I could see the flooded fields by the River Severn. Somewhere in the flood was the Offa's Dyke path which after a while joined the canal path along with the Severn Way before veering back out into the flood lands. I stuck to the dry towpath which being on a bank was raised up above the floods.

A sign indicated a pub 100 metres off the canal path, I went to warm up and buy a pot of tea. The bartender looked bored, looking at his phone, he came over to chat. He was from the Philippines and enjoyed walking. He missed the sea though and also his dog had recently died. He also missed his family who he had not been able to visit for a couple of years because of covid. His plan was to visit them in the autumn. I felt privileged to be able to travel and see family and friends, covid-19 had prevented so many families from getting together. I thought too of all the displaced people who are never able to return to their homelands, I had been able to walk through all my past easily.

Near Wern a local lady was out checking the flood height, she lived in a nearby farm which was okay as a few years earlier they had raised the floors by three feet. She said a neighbour flooded every year. I came to a picnic site, the wind was strong but I tucked my tent in by a bridge away from any trees and on a less wet patch of grass. It turned out to be a popular evening dog walking area, one dog barked loudly at my closed tent. I had a chat with the owner through the 'canvas', he asked if I had enough food as he had some porridge sachets in his van! Perhaps I should have said 'yes please' as I woke in the night hungry and so lay in my sleeping bag eating bread. I was struggling to eat enough calories walking and camping.

The next day dawned calm and dry, birdsong filled the air. Two kingfishers flew along the canal, emerald jewels against the sombre colours of the winter vegetation, though their russet breasts gave camouflage when they perched. Eventually they reached the extent of their territory and darted back past me. A heron rose 'cronking' from the bank and tree creepers circled the tree trunks. Moorhen emerged from the reeds, their red heads and white tail feathers adding a splash of colour. Soon heavy rain set in and by the time I reached Llanymynech, five miles away, I was cold and wet so glad to see a small café and go in for a second breakfast. A man in his early thirties at a nearby table told how he used to go out walking but now didn't have the time. He seemed sad about that fact and I hoped he could find the time.

Rain had turned to sleet as I left. I walked past some poor looking houses whose windows were right on the pavement. Through the net curtains there were glimpses in to front rooms where electric fires were giving out heat, an expensive way to heat a house. They had old sash windows too. I felt sorry for the occupants as large lorries passed by making it pointless cleaning the windows and letting more light in.

Climbing up through woodland once more on the Offa's Dyke path, it began to snow. A group of volunteers were busy clearing scrubland to make way for wild flowers. They had lit a smoky fire to burn the waste, one man said they had not expected snow so would finish early. Soon everywhere was white and quite pretty looking, though also very slippery so that when I reached a road I decided to follow that to Trefonen rather than the longer Offa's Dyke route via hills and fields. It was not the best decision as the road was busy and the cars covered me with wet slush. By the time I reached Trefonen the snow had changed to rain and I was cold and wet. It was Saturday, a group of children had come out sledging. In a garden two children were building a snowman.

It was too cold to stop long, I sheltered in a bus stop, the interior decorated with paintings by the local children. I re-joined the Offa's Dyke path climbing up through extensive woodland to arrive at a snow covered old race course above Oswestry. The sun had emerged and lots of people had driven up to enjoy the snow. The land lower down was bare and dark looking compared to the white of the snow. The rest of the day was sunny as I walked through sheep fields and descended down to Craignant where I hoped to camp. It is a very narrow, tree filled valley with a scattering of houses on the Welsh-English border, there was nowhere to camp. I saw some flat grass across the track from a house so knocked to check if it was alright to camp there. The lady came out and suggested I went half a mile back along the road to a farm where there had been a campsite about ten years ago. A very active old lady came to the door there, she looked about 75 but it turned out she was 88 and had given up the campsite when she was 77! Her son and her were happy for me to camp on their field, just concerned that the ground was wet. She showed me where the toilet was and said she would leave the backdoor unlocked in case I got "taken short" in the night. I was very grateful I could camp there as I did not want to continue any further and it was also sheltered in the valley.

It was as well I did not go up to the house until 7am in the morning as the dog barked, it was being very good and had a cosy kennel under the carport. I packed up and left about 8am, the lady waving from the kitchen window. I vigorously waved my thanks, I never even learnt her name. Later I realised that she was in Wales, the lady who had directed me there was in England....

The rain continued as I made my way to the canal at Chirk cutting down country lanes which were traffic free early on the Sunday morning. At the Ceiriog river I met the Shropshire Way which led me under the impressive Chirk aqueduct and railway viaduct but I wanted to be up above on the towpath. I scrambled up the steep bank, climbed over the fence and there was the canal. A man came along with a small rucksack and said a few words about escaping from the house then disappeared into the canal tunnel. I checked my phone and answered concerned texts from friends and family as to how I was managing in the storms and then walked into the tunnel too, then turned round again. The tunnel is 421metres long with a bend in it and no lights, there was no sign of light at the end of the tunnel. I opted to walk above it on the road, I presume the man came out the other end, I never saw him.

I re-joined the towpath and walked to Froncysyllte where there is a high, long aqueduct over the valley. Walkers have two options following the Offa's Dyke path here of either crossing the aqueduct or going via the road which drops down into the valley and then climbs back up again. I was considering crossing the aqueduct but the strength of the wind gave me visions of being blown into the canal or worse so I opted for the road to Trevor. I wanted to find a toilet but the public toilets were closed, I enquired at the visitor's centre and they directed me to the Chapel café. Were all the toilets out of action or was it a clever ploy on the part of the café which on this Sunday morning was busy with customers. I felt slightly guilty sitting in a chapel, now café, drinking tea on a Sunday especially as on the Isle of Lewis most places are closed on a Sunday. A family on holiday at the next table had saved a sausage and a slice of black pudding on a plate to take back to their dog who was unwell, rather a dubious diet for a sick dog!

The rain had eased off as I left to follow the roads to Ruabon where I picked up the Wat's Dyke path which I followed the six miles to Wrexham. I don't know who Wat was but he built a bank and dug a ditch or rather his minions did, the same as Offa. Leaders were in to constructing such things then rather like constructing the canals in the eighteenth century, railways in the nineteenth and motorways in the twentieth. In many ways they all served the same purpose; to prevent people moving between areas and control movement in certain directions as well as to control the masses by setting them to work. This section of the Wat's Dyke path could be a nice route except for the numerous broken or overgrown stiles. At the edge of Wrexham it enters Erddig park, owned by the National Trust and despite the now heavy rain people were out walking. I was disappointed the route did not give views of the half-timbered house there but it skirts below the gardens and wall. The edge of Wrexham has large houses but nearer the centre the place looked run-down. As I headed through town to the station the rain became worse and the wind stronger until the full force of Storm Franklin hit. It was with great relief that I jumped on the rail replacement bus to Chester. I was completely soaked to the skin and somewhere enroute the wind had stolen my waterproof rucksack cover, so apologies to the people of Wrexham for littering their town. By the time we reached Chester we had left the storm behind. I only had a few minutes to spare to jump on the train to Bebington where my father-in-law collected me for some time out before the next stage of my walk

Chapter 9

Wirral to Edale; mud, canals & Pennine Way
21st -26th Feb

I spent a couple of days with my in-laws which gave me a chance to rest and sort things out for the next stage of my walk. I had sent a parcel on to them containing a guide to the Pennine Way and sections of maps for the rest of my walk, including all of my planned route through Scotland plus gaiters in-case of snow further north and a couple of pairs of socks. The parcel felt quite weighty and looking at all the extra additions to be carried it was too much, things needed to be rationalised. Completely emptying out my rucksack I re-considered what I was carrying. Could the maps perhaps be sent to where I needed them beyond the Pennine Way? I could pick them up at the Border Hotel in Kirk Yetholm at the end of that section. I rang the hotel and they were quite happy with that. I was still carrying trainers and running clothes but intended to post them home after running a parkrun in Sheffield. I did though post home the maps I had been using since the forest and a towel I had been carrying. I was also able to fully dry out my tent, it is surprising just how much heavier a wet tent is.

I also re-evaluated my future plans as originally I had planned to walk the Pennine Way in twelve and a half days starting on a Saturday after parkrun and finishing in time to get to a parkrun in Kelso two weeks later. This would mean walking over twenty miles a number of days. Looking at the cicerone guide again it suggests taking sixteen to twenty days, much more realistic. Martha was planning to walk with me for the first six days which meant we could comfortably reach Horton. A good place for Mary, my youngest daughter, to meet us as she and Martha were then planning a few days away together. After that I could take as long as I liked to reach the end, I would forget about the Kelso parkrun and allow time to rest or stop for a day if the weather became very bad. I was apprehensive about the Pennine Way, it is over 260 miles through challenging uplands.

Two days later I caught a train to Chester and then to Frodsham to join the North Cheshire Way which I roughly planned to follow to Edale. It had been raining as I left the Wirral but in Frodsham the sun was shining and I hoped no more storms were coming. I had chosen Frodsham to join the North Cheshire Way as I thought it would be easy to join it there except I started heading the opposite direction! My confusion was partly because I was now heading east instead of west so needed to have the sun on my right-hand side, not my left. The way is also poorly marked and initially went through very wet fields of rye grass or horse fields before meeting the river Weaver. Ironically once beside the river there were more way markers, when there was no other way to go! Old woodland lined the river, dog's mercury and ransomes were just beginning to emerge. It was as well it wasn't raining as I could see how high the water had been, the path would have been flooded.

At Dutton lock the river becomes a canal and I met firm

tracks and people out walking. On my left were 'no entry' signs; 'danger deep mud, dredging pits'. Signs like that would have been useful for the muddy sheep fields on the Offa's Dyke!

At Sullerton locks are two attractive lock houses, the lock-keeper was throwing a ball for his collie. He said how lovely it was living in the lock keeper's house and how in the summer the lock was full of boats. It was a lovely spot by the canal. In Barnton I met Christina sitting in the sun by her house which faces the canal. I asked if she could fill up my water bottle and eventually left an hour later after a lovely chat, sitting in the sun with a pot of tea and biscuits. She said how she had been unwell and walking along the canal was helping her recovery. It is possible to walk along canals from Barnston all the way to Bristol, which was her goal. She said how much she liked living by the canal and meeting people. As if to prove the point a local man stopped for a chat, his dog was called Bill. My mood became cheerful again as I had been feeling fed up after a detour to an uninspiring shop in Barnston along a busy, litter lined road.

I walked past the Anderton boat lift. Built in 1875 it raises boats vertically 50feet from the Trent and Mersey canal up to the river Weaver navigation and is only one of two boat lifts in the country. Unfortunately the visitors centre was closed and the boat lift was partly hidden behind trees to get a good view of it which was a shame. A little bit further on I found a patch of grass to pitch my tent. A man in a nearby house visited to check me out and then told me about the area. It is where underground brine is extracted and then sent to Runcorn to be processed, yet another salt area. I had noticed large pipes crossing the canal. The brine extraction can cause issues and sometimes sections of the canal collapse. His row of houses had been built in 1882 for the brine workers. As he walked away he said to knock if I needed anything in the night. He was not the first person to say that to me at my camp spots, I met so many kind people.

Further along the canal there was more industry but as I passed an old house the next morning an elderly man was coming out with his mug of tea and a chair to sit in the sun. He would be looking at a chemical works but I had the impression he was content and was enjoying his home. I thought about the places I'd walked through which were not particularly scenic but where the local people were out enjoying what was on offer.

I was walking through the brine industry area and had to negotiate some very busy roads. Yet by the railway and access track to industry were some beautiful tall silver birch trees and I watched three greater spotted woodpeckers squabbling, their red crowns adding colour to the woods. There often seemed to be more wildlife in the more built-up areas, the 'accidental countryside' as written about by Stephen Moss.

Walking through the village of Plumley I played with the name in my head, rhyming it with Lumley. The village turned out to be as lovely as it sounds. Daffodils bloomed on the verges, the shop was well stocked, a smiling older lady ran past and a litter pick was organised for the next Sunday. A dog walker said it was impossible to be lonely in Plumley.

It was a muddy walk to cross the M6 motorway to Knutsford where the trees had taken a battering from the storms. A massive beech tree lay like a fallen leviathan. The force of its fall had split the trunk, the orange 'flesh' a shocking scar against the grey trunk. A lot of the houses had equally large trees in their gardens, which seemed rather scary. It began raining and I had to negotiate a lot of muddy horse fields and getting to yet another stile into yet another churned up field I gave up. A farmer in a tractor pointed out a sandy track I could walk along instead to get to the same end point. I moaned about the state of the fields but he said how it was cruel to stable horses all winter and that walkers should expect mud! Adding that he had to work and couldn't go off walking, I beat a hasty retreat.

The rain had stopped by the time I arrived in Alderley Edge so I was able to sit a while on a bench and eat before the rain restarted and sent me into the shops. Leaving town I realised I had forgotten to buy water so I knocked on a door. The lady looked puzzled and scared, shutting the door when she took my bottle to fill up. It was raining hard when she returned it full and she said she hoped I was going home as it was too wet to walk! I didn't want to point out that if I was going home I wouldn't have needed water.

The rain soon stopped as I headed up on to Alderley Edge completely losing the North Cheshire Way signs. There were signs for a donkey trek route, I wouldn't have minded a donkey to carry my pack. It is strange with a rucksack as some days I would barely notice it but other days it would be irritating my hip bones or digging into my left shoulder. It of course was always heavier at the end of the day when I had stocked up with food and water and that was when I was more tired. Heading in what I hoped was the right direction I realised I could see the start of the Pennines, covered with a thin layer of snow. I found a dryish spot on a wide area of footpath to camp and listened to the owls and the honking of geese, grazing on the wet rye grass fields.

Shortly after setting off the next day I arrived at a golf course which was a bit disappointing as I had been thinking that the edge of a golf course would make a very good camp spot. Nice short, level grass and quiet! I would need to get up early though to avoid golf balls. I walked past massive new houses with tennis courts and security fencing, the wealth of Cheshire. The North Cheshire Way led me through yet more very wet sheep fields before, oh joy, meeting the Macclesfield canal. I like canals, they are easy walking with no stiles, pleasant scenery and you can't get lost. I couldn't help peeping into the houseboats as I went past, a glimpse of another life; a woman lying on her bed reading, an older lady and child playing on the floor, an old man sitting at a table amongst piles of papers, stoves glowing warm, sending up smoke. I rather hoped I would be invited in one day for a mug of tea.

The morning sun had gone and it began to snow as I entered Lyme park. The North Cheshire Way skirts the edge of the park taking walkers over bleak moorland, I opted for a scenic route along tree lined tracks through the park. A young child with his mother was having fun hiding behind trees and climbing the banks. Around a corner red deer were relaxing with snow covered backs. Then I saw the large car-park by Lyme house and had to smile as there at a picnic bench sat a group of brightly clothed people resolutely finishing their picnic in the snow!

As I headed to the exit I could see the tower blocks of Manchester and leaving the park at Disley I was suddenly in the North of England. Somewhere in Lyme park I had left Middle England. The landscape had changed to moorland with dry stone walls and dark stone houses. It was canal walking again to head east towards the Peak district via the Peak Forest canal. This ends at Bugsworth basin where the Polish warden sells hot drinks and home-made cakes from his barge. A large container makes a comfy place to sit in and read the information boards on the walls. Beyond is the Peak Forest tramway where a group of children ahead of their mothers were having a great time jumping in the puddles, getting completely drenched. It was good to see children out having fun, I often noticed a lack of children when I did see people walking.

I detoured to the shop in Chinley to buy food for the first three days of the Pennine Way. The helpful owners were assisting an old man to get his shopping, he then set off along the pavement with his zimmer frame in canvas shoes and no coat despite the squally snow showers! Two teenage girls walked down the road in skimpy leggings and bare ankles, same as teenagers everywhere. I was beginning to feel overdressed in boots and full waterproofs.

I had worried about the final section to Edale as it is over open moorland and I set out prepared with map, compass and whistle. Would I need to pick a route? I laughed when I discovered a sign post and a clear path over the hills to Edale, of course this is a heavily walked area, not northern Scotland. A sprinkling of snow covered the hills and I glanced nervously at Kinder Scout hoping visibility would be good for crossing it the next day. I know Edale a bit from visits there when my youngest daughter, Mary, worked at the youth hostel and I had heard tales of the cloud on Kinder Scout. But that was tomorrows worry, for today the sun shone and I was having a rest as I had arranged to go to a friend in Sheffield for the night. At Edale I went into the station café to celebrate the end of the southern section of my walk and also the end of six weeks walking, meaning I was half way through time-wise. The café sells excellent cakes. I wandered into the village to take a 'selfie' in front of the Nag's Head pub and its board announcing the official start of the Pennine Way. The sun was shining, it could be raining the next day.

I caught the train to Jane and Gordon's in Sheffield and had a relaxing afternoon and evening with them before Martha eventually arrived at 9.30pm having travelled direct from the island for an early start the next day.

Chapter 10

Edale to Horton; reservoirs, sun & rain

26th Feb-3rd March

We had planned to run the local parkrun but it would mean a late start from Edale so we decided not to. It is also an uninspiring three lap out and back course along narrow park paths. It looked very busy as we drove past the next day enroute to the station to catch the little two coach train to Edale.

When my sister was at Durham university in the early 1980's she had suggested that we walk the Pennine Way one summer, an ambitious idea as I had never seen moorland and neither of us had experience of long-distance walking. We planned to stay in youth hostels but our mother had discouraged us with tales of it being one big bog. In retrospect I find that amusing as she had never been north of York at the time. Recently reading John Burn's account of his Pennine Way walk in 1972 she was probably correct. He recounts falling headlong into black peaty bogs and rescuing a Dutch man who had sunk up to his waist in the wet peat. John Hillaby also tells of the peat and bogs at the start of the Pennine Way. This was in the early days of the route before it had been improved with stone slabs marking the way over the worst of the bogs.

I was excited to now be walking the Pennine Way, but also apprehensive, it is 268miles. I was worried about what the weather would throw at me. So far, apart from the storms, the weather had been good but I was aware it was still winter and I was heading north. Also having struggled on the Offa's Dyke would I find it so much harder on an entirely upland walk? I was also not sure how well the route would be signposted and so how much navigation is needed.

The sun was shining though as we got off the packed train in Edale with the promise of a couple of days of dry weather. Martha took photos of me by the gate across the road from the Nag's Head which also claims to be the official start of the Pennine Way! We set off up the track along with fifty other people, a bit of a shock after weeks of walking alone. A party of twenty kept on stopping, then overtaking, one of their group had a radio playing loudly. We decided to stop for a while to let them get ahead and after a while the crowds spread out. The walking turned out simple, up the stone steps of Jacob's ladder on to the plateau and a clear route round the edge and over to the Snake Pass. The only difficulty I found was negotiating all the rocks as I do not find rocks easy to walk on. There are some curious rock formations along the way formed by wind and rain erosion. We crossed an empty road at the Snake Pass as it was closed due to landslides and then walked over Bleak Low, which lives up to its name. The bog is crossed though on stone slabs so not difficult but it was a long day and the sun was setting pink as we descended in to the valley before Torside and looked for a camp spot.

The next day dawned clear and cold, the ground solid but the wind had kept the tents from freezing and so they were dry to pack away. It was to be an easy day walking over vast open moorlands and beside reservoirs which added interest to an otherwise bleak landscape. I was glad to have company, anyone walking this section alone I would advise to either have a good book to read or headphones. It felt strange to be in such bleak emptiness but within sight of Manchester and other urban areas and also the soaring concrete mast at Emley Moor. Climbing up on to the vast emptiness of Black Hill we saw a man lying there on his CB radio. It reminded us of years ago when we met four men at a hostel in the Outer Hebrides who were CB radio fanatics. They were chartering boats to go out and broadcast from uninhabited islands.

It was warm in the sun, if out of the wind and at Dean Clough a young woman with purple and blue dyed hair was sitting bare foot in the yoga position by the river. She looked very peaceful and I thought how nice to walk over the moor from the car park and relax there. The North is so different to the South having such wild areas near to where large numbers of people live. It was Sunday so where the paths were good families were out walking and there were lots of runners.

At Standedge we left the Pennine Way to join the Pennine bridleway and dropped down to Castle Shaw Upper reservoir to camp. It wasn't that easy to find a reasonably sheltered, flattish spot, the ground was hard to get the pegs in to so we used rocks as well. It was a lovely evening, we were able to lie in the late sun until 5pm, when the cold sent us in to our tents. I rang my sister, Sarah, who for the past thirty years had lived in Russia making her home near Moscow and raising her four children there. The past week newspaper headlines had been about the threatened invasion of the Ukraine by Russia and suddenly everything had escalated. Now Sarah was telling us that she was planning to leave

Russia and come to Britain while it was still possible to leave. It felt like 1939, she was planning to leave the next week and send her youngest daughter in a few days time to Anna's in London.

We woke to rain, which was disappointing. It became increasingly heavy throughout the day, which didn't help with the bleakness of the route. It is the bleakest section of the Pennine Way as the moorland is so vast and void of trees. We crossed the M62 on a high concrete bridge looking at the traffic creeping along. I commented that it is still quieter than the M20 and Martha said that in some ways the motorway added to the landscape rather than being detrimental to the scenery. Later a series of reservoirs added variety to the landscape. We had a rest just before Soudley Pike monument where a small stone seat, in memory of some walker, gives a welcome shelter from the wind and rain. The view may be great but we could see little. Martha tried to remember the route as she had run that way on the 30 mile Haworth Hobble race. Soudley Pike is a monstrosity of a structure in dark stone to commemorate peace after the Battle of Waterloo. We could have sheltered in its base but it felt very overpowering.

We descended down, down and down to Hebden Bridge which is in the bottom of a very deep, dark valley. Tall, former mill houses and chimneys are squeezed in along the road and canal, it felt very claustrophobic. We popped in to the co op and then headed out up the hill, passing half a dozen white geese grazing the grass in front of the Methodist church on the main street. We had booked an air bnb in Heptonstall which is on the hill top above. We had looked across at the church perched on the edge of the hillside before we descended to Hebden Bridge. To get there involved a climb up steep stone steps and then a very steep path through woods to emerge in the village. It feels like stepping back in time to arrive there; the houses are built on the very edge of the steep drop and are old stone, weavers' houses facing cobbled streets, everything huddled together. The bnb was an old three storey house on a narrow cobbled street with flower pots by the door in lieu of a garden. It was good to get in out of the rain and remove wet clothes and gear. My waterproofs had leaked so absolutely everything I was wearing was wet. We sorted out our things and I packed up my trainers and running clothes which I had saved for the parkrun. I should have sent them home after the forest of dean parkrun, I had carried them a long way unnecessarily. The tiny shop-cum-post office was just down the road, it turned out that a man there had owned a house in Stornoway! I bought a newspaper to stuff in our boots and to spread on the floor to catch the drips from our coats.

We were worried about the news that all the European flights from Russia had been stopped, things were changing very rapidly. Would Sarah and Varya be able to leave? We phoned the rest of the family and learnt that they were enroute to St Petersburgh by train and hoping to be able to travel via Finland, but would that border remain open? It felt very surreal, in January when I started my walk I was worried about the omicron version of covid and whether restrictions would be increased. Covid was no longer in the news and England had lifted all restrictions, although some places, such as Heptonstall post office still requested you wore a face-mask and limited the number of people inside. Ukraine was all the news now, my sister and niece were about to escape their country. I felt guilty walking.

Shirley our bnb host is lovely, she had asked if we wanted bacon and egg butties for breakfast. We of course had not refused and went down in the morning to find two butties each plus cereals. We chatted for a while before she left for work. As she was leaving she said she'd made some buns, opening a tin to reveal home-made fairy cakes and offering us one each. That made a nice addition to our mid-morning break. We washed up then left. The sun shone in a blue sky, we decided to explore Heptonstall for a while. It is all stone houses and very peaceful but good to see lived in by families, lots of children were being walked to the local school. I contrasted it to the empty Cotswold villages with no families and many second homes. There is an octagonal Methodist chapel, the only one of that design and the oldest chapel continuously used. The parish church is very imposing with a ruined church next-door. Shirley had told us that Heptonstall is famous as Shirley Plath is buried here. I had to confess to not knowing who she was and so was told she had been married to Ted Hughes which left me none the wiser. Her grave is well visited and messages are left on it.

Following along the edge of the valley we re-joined the main Pennine Way, resisting the temptation of detouring to May's shop. The sign announced 'sells owt tha wants'. We soon met three Yorkshire ladies. They asked if we were walking the Pennine Way and were surprised we were camping so we confessed to having stayed in a bnb in Heptonstall, "ah, where Sylvia Plath is buried" they replied.

It was a lovely varied days walk in sunshine. We stopped by Walshall Dean Lower reservoir for our first break, sitting with our backs against the wall to be in the sun but out of the cold wind.At Top Withens, the inspiration for Wuthering Heights a lady was reading a leather-bound version of the book. Atleast we presumed that was what she was reading, it may have been a D.H.Lawrence. We were now on the tourist route from Haworth, the signs are in English and Japanese! At Ponden reservoir I switched on my phone to discover a text confirming Sarah and Varya had made it to Finland and were enroute to London, they were free but had left with just an hour to pack belongings in a suitcase each.

We walked over heather covered moorland which must look beautiful late summer when in flower. Before Ickornshaw we came across an empty, old stone house by a stream and set up camp. It was out of sight of houses and we felt as if we were back on the island next to the 'airighs' in the north at Ness (they are summer huts). It was a peaceful camp spot. The next day we discovered that there were lots of huts, presumably summer 'escapes' though oddly they were not marked on the map. We had woken to a damp misty day and it was to be wet all day and tough walking as we dropped down in to the gap between the moors and the limestone country. We walked through sheep fields which meant lots of stone stiles over walls with mini-wooden gates on top to prevent sheep jumping over. These gates are very common on the Pennine Way and often have strong springs to close them so I had to develop a technique of not letting go of the gate before both legs and walking poles were clear.

Nearing Ickornshaw we came across fifty plus cockerels and hens perched in a yard by a run-down house. There were a couple of cars and an old caravan filled with sacks and rubbish but the birds looked healthy with glossy coats. Officially all poultry were supposed to be undercover away from wild birds because of avian flu.

On Pinhaw moor is a new view indicator, not that we had a view. It incorporated a memorial to all those who died in the covid-19 epidemic as well as to Robert Wilson who was a beacon man during the Napoleonic wars. He died on the moor during a snow storm, and is buried nearby. It was ironic that the moorland gave easy walking where as the lowland was a nightmare through wet, soggy rye grass fields. In the early days of the Pennine Way this section would have been a respite from the bogs on the moors. Early accounts of walking the way also describe buying food at farmhouses, I have never tried asking at a farm for food but I am not sure whether they would provide the meals they used to.

We slithered over wet, muddy fields to Gargrave where a man from Kent extolled the virtues of his adopted town; its river, shops, railway, location… Gargrave is nice, we bought sausage and bean pasties to give us the energy for another six miles to Malham, noting they contained 80% of your recommended daily allowance of fat, we needed it. There is also the Dalesman café, an old- fashioned sweetshop cum café but we didn't want to linger long so didn't treat ourselves. Martha photographed me by the sign outside, 186miles Kirk Yetholm, 70 miles Edale which she pointed out meant I was less than a third of the way along the Pennine Way. I retorted that I was almost 600 miles from Ramsgate so half way through my walk.

I really struggled along the next six miles to Malham. I would happily have stopped for the night in Gargrave but that would have meant more mileage the next day. The rain fell harder and the fields were slippier. At Hanlith we abandoned the Pennine Way, which climbs up again, and took the flatter route to Malham by the river. It was gone 5.30pm when we saw the cliff of Malham cove emerging through the mist and found a perfect camp spot beside the stream at Aird Head.

It was still damp and misty the next morning but not cold. It was Martha's last day with me and we were aiming for Horton to meet Mary who was driving down. I had rung up to book us into the campsite at Horton. When I rang in the evening the old man who answered said I was to ring again in the morning as he did not have the bookings book on him

"I am 83 and have gone to roost"

What a wonderful image! With the wet we decided to

change plans and book into the bunkhouse at the back of the Golden Lion instead as camping with three people in the rain is not much fun. We texted Mary to instruct her to bring food to cook.

Malham was quiet early morning before the day trippers, it is an attractive village and the limestone scenery is spectacular. We had camped here before by Gordale scar, the camp site run by an eccentric local with a hoarding habit; he went through all rubbish storing it up around the house, resulting in piles of air beds and gas cylinders as well as mugs of tooth brushes in the washroom!

Despite the mist and the damp the walk that day was lovely, first to Malham cove which becomes more impressive the closer you get to it. It is the highest inland cliff in Britain. I avoided the slippery limestone pavement on top, we saw a lone walker who I was to meet a few times in the next few days.

We followed the rocky valley towards Malham tarn where a group of young children were being taught about rivers. Further on more children were in the yard at Malham field centre. It is in a great location by the tarn with a long, wooded drive, lined with carved wooden birds. There were no views all day apart from close up glimpses of drystone pavements and walls. We passed some isolated, high up hill farms. Before Horton the Pennine Way detours over Pen-y-Ghent, which was barely visible. I had climbed it in 1988 and remembered a big boggy hill and did suggest we by-passed it but Martha wanted to climb it. Now a good stone path climbs up to the summit and stone steps descend the other side but without them it would be boggy. There was no view from the top. Blondine (who we had seen at Malham cove) caught us up on the summit, she was walking the Pennine Way as far as Alston and staying indoors so we let her go ahead at a faster pace with her lighter pack.

The rain had stopped by the time we reached Horton which is a small farming community with a church and two pubs by the River Ribble. Years ago on a long car journey to Scotland we had made up rhymes about the River Ribble as we crossed it. Every word had to start with an 'R', it was interesting to now look down on the river itself. I wanted some eggs so we left our things in the bunkhouse in search of the shop, it had closed down but we found a house selling eggs. We popped in to the church which appeared well used. I was amused by a photo of sheep in the church porch with a bible text from Ezekiel below 'The Lord will judge the fat sheep from the scrawny sheep' it kept me smiling for days.

Mary arrived with lots of food so we cooked a good meal of pasta with a stir fry of fresh veg, the first proper dinner for six days. I was also able to ring Sarah, now safely at Anna's in London, but worryingly her married daughter was still in Moscow unable to leave yet, and her son had chosen to stay too. Sanctions were now being imposed on Russia and the situation was worse. The Ukraine was being bombed and invaded, the world was changing. I said I felt guilty walking but Sarah replied that I should walk and expressed great interest in how far I had got and what everything was like.

Chapter 11

Horton to Dufton; sun, barns and waterfalls

4th-8th March

Breakfast in Horton was a big affair; bacon on croissants and scrambled egg on toast, I felt like a camel stocking up for the week ahead. Mary and Martha accompanied me to the other end of the village where the Pennine Way turns off the road at the Crown Inn. They were to meet me in five days time in Dufton on their way back home. The weather was good and the route lovely as I headed up an old track between dry stone walls. This is limestone country full of sink holes and swallow holes where water has dissolved the rock. I climbed over a wall at one swallow hole to see the gushing river disappear in to the ground down a gaping, rocky hole. I wondered how many sheep also disappear underground as there were no fences to stop them and recalled a tragic account of how a hen had disappeared in an underground stream in India and how three men were lost in an attempt to rescue the hen and then the men...

At Ling Gill Beck there is a very narrow, deep, tree filled

ravine which is fenced in to protect the trees as a reserve. The trees were thick and obscured any view of the stream. It is a shame more areas are not fenced off to allow trees to grow. After that there is a wide track on to Cam Fell with views down to patches of forestry and isolated hill farms in the valleys below. It became cold, as I entered clouds, the Pennine Way climbs up to 580metres. I put on gloves as the mist came down and the temperature dropped.

Descending out of the mist I looked down into Wensleydale which is full of stone barns and drystone walls. The small town of Hawes is the highest market town in Britain. It was hard to believe there was a town as somehow Hawes remains concealed, hidden by trees and a ridge in the land. I had hoped to be able to leave my tent at a camp site to explore the town but sites were either closed or did not take tents. Hawes is an interesting town full of small independent shops including another old-fashioned sweet shop – they like their sweeties in Yorkshire!

Continuing out of town through sheep fields to Hardraw I met a farmer with five collies. He commented on my pack and I said I was looking for somewhere to camp to which he said I could camp in his field, which was great as I could shelter by the stone wall. He recounted how a few years previously he had come across an older man camping in the snow during 'the Beast from the East'. The man had stayed until the summer helping to repair stone walls and came back each year. It was a good camp spot, I listened to barn owls calling for mates and in the morning visited the young pigs snoring in the barn. I wondered if they went in to the locally reared pork pies sold in the spar deli in Hawes. They were small, ball shaped pies and I imagined them to be a domesticated beastie similar to haggis cooked in pastry instead of in their skins. These pigs looked very content snuggled up together on deep straw, snoring. One was awake watching me through a half-open eye but didn't get up. Looking at the Cicerone guide I realised there is a picture of the barn and field on the cover.

The sun shone after a hard frost as I set out for Great Shunner Fell, a name I enjoyed saying in my head, though by now on my walk it may have been out loud. It was the start of week eight of my walk and I felt good. My feet and heels no longer hurt and I was enjoying the simple routine of walking and camping. I was also thoroughly enjoying the Pennine Way and wondering why I had been so anxious about it. Apart from the first couple of days the scenery had been amazing and I was enjoying seeing new places. I was not familiar with this area of Britain, having only visited it once many years previously. My walk was now about heading North, I had no one else to visit and no more visiting my past except for a planned detour to St Andrews in Scotland where I went to university and a visit to a friend in Edinburgh, but that was a while away.

Curlew and lapwing flew up as I climbed up on to the fells. The views were superb and I could see Pen-y-Ghent and also Ingleside, two of the Yorkshire three peaks (the third being Whernside, however I wasn't sure which way to look for it). Great Shunner Fell rises to 716m so is mountain height, there was a cold north wind. I pulled my tube up over my face but the sun was out and the path good. In places the water was iced up over the stone slabs so I was glad of my walking poles to break the ice to make foot holes. The stone slabs which are used extensively on the Pennine Way have been recycled, some showing where the metal posts of railings once were. Ton bags of slabs waiting to be laid were there on the moor. Patches of snow lay around and further north some fells were completely white. At the summit is a multi-sided shelter with seats so I was able to sit in the sun, but out of the wind to rest and eat.

The descent to Thwaite in Swaledale was long, I took it slowly as my knee was twinging. I think it was a nerve reacting to my heavier pack having stocked up with food in Hawes. I was slightly annoyed with myself as I could have left some things with the girls and collected them in Dufton; I had for instance a new gas bottle for further north which Mary had brought me. Hunting in my pack for a knee bandage support I discovered a solitary, stale wrap lurking at the bottom. I don't even like wraps and had only bought a packet quite a while previously as there was nothing else to buy. I broke it up and left it on the moor, a treat for the wildlife. I resolved to rationalise my pack when I reached Dufton.

Swaledale is beautiful, full of preserved stone barns with stone tiled roofs. They had been built in every field to house the cows with hay lofts above. It made me think of the Alps and Heidi. Thwaite sadly is mostly holiday homes and the café was up for sale. I went in for a pot of tea which came with a large home-made ginger biscuit. A leaflet advertised a woollen centre a couple of miles away in another village and samples of beautiful Swaledale knitwear were in the window. It would have been interesting to visit the place but a two mile detour would mean an extra four miles walking, a couple of hours timewise. The disadvantage of being on foot, in a car it would be an easy detour. Two women arrived who had also walked over from Hawes following my footprints over Great Shunner Fell. They must have had cold feet as they were wearing trainers but they were returning to Hawes youth hostel via the road. As I was leaving Blondine arrived, she was heading for the pub in Keld for the night.

It is an impressive route to Keld above the steep, rocky slopes of the valley. I met a couple on a circular route from Keld, they were doing day walks along the Pennine

Way with the intention of eventually covering the entire length that way. Of course that means doing circular walks to return to the car so they would only have walked two miles of the actual Pennine Way that day. I found myself trying to calculate how many days it would therefore take to cover the whole Pennine Way and gave up, coming to the conclusion it would take a very long time.

I camped just before Keld by a noisy and impressive waterfall (according to the 'Dalesman' magazine the river Swale is the fastest river in the UK), then wandered in to the village. It is a tiny place of ancient stone houses. There is a welcoming sign at the public hall 'self-service winter café, tea room, cakes'. I went in to be greeted by several walkers sitting by a log fire in a wood-panel lined room with well-stocked bookshelves. The kitchen area had a kettle with a large selection of teas, coffee, squashes and oh joy, six tins of home-made cakes. I was spoilt for choice but plumped for Yorkshire brack, a substantial tea loaf. The day walkers suggested I could sleep in the hall, I pointed out that if I did there would be no cake left. The weather was good but had it been raining I may well have stayed in for the night. They kindly donated enough for myself too as I had left my money back at the tent. I rather fell in love with Keld, partly because of the cakes but also the scenery is so beautiful, although it did feel slightly like a museum and is probably very busy in the summer.

It was sunny again the next day as I left Keld to the accompaniment of birds – gulls, curlews, tumbling peewits and even oyster catchers, which I thought only lived at the coast. It is a pleasant moorland walk to the highest pub in Britain, Tan Hill at 530m. It is where the Penine Way enters county Durham. It was very busy there with lots of motor homes parked up outside and some campers, a cold windy spot. I went in for a coffee and as I left I could see Blondine approaching about half a mile away. I didn't wait as she would catch me up and I was surprised she had not left earlier as she was planning on walking much further than me that day.

The next section was all bog, picking a way from marker post to marker post, one of the worse sections of the Pennine Way. Arriving at a track I waited for Blondine, approaching through the bog, so we could walk a while together. We talked of her plans to move to her parents' property in France and grow veg. When we turned off the track I let her go on ahead wishing her well for the rest of her walk.

County Durham is rounded hills and wide valleys. I like the Durham dales they felt more lived in and less touristy than Yorkshire. The A66 dual carriageway cuts through one valley right beside farmhouses. It was sad to come across lots of rubbish by the underpass yet I also stood and watched the changing patterns of a murmuration of starlings above the road. I thought about my walk and the places I had visited, where I had lived and thought of all the refugees who are unable to return to the place of their birth. I felt grateful to have been born in Britain and to have the freedom I was enjoying.

It was warm in the sun, I stopped by a stream to lie on a flat rock and enjoy the warmth. I was on a grouse moor devoid of birds despite a notice stating

'Bowes moor was designated a site of special scientific interest in 1989 and now local farmers, owners of shooting rights and English nature manage it to get the correct balance and maintain a moor'.

A rather controversial statement in view of the lack of birds over the moorland compared to the numerous birds on the rough grazing nearby.

I pitched my tent by the river at Baldersdale and sat in the sun until 5pm. Later I left the tent to walk to 'Hannah's meadow' nature reserve. Years ago I had read a book about Hannah Hauxwell who was 'discovered' in the 1970's by the BBC making a documentary about farms in the north. She was living extremely simply with one cow at Low Birk Hatt, her meadows had never been sprayed and so are species rich. Two of the meadows are now nature reserves but in early March there were no flowers and they looked the same as everywhere else, which was rather disappointing. I am sure they look lovely in the summer. I did look in the barn which houses some old tools and has some information boards. I met the lady who now lives in Hannah's old house and we spoke about how isolated she was then. Now she says it is quick to get into town and she has many friends in the local community. By the time I got back to my tent it was almost dark, a crescent moon had risen and the sky was clear. The temperature had plummeted and frost was forming on my tent. I put on another woollen jumper.

It was a very cold night, the coldest on the trip so far, the tent stiff with frost in the morning. I woke to sunshine and as I set off through sheep fields sky larks were singing and washing hung on the lines by the farmhouses. I passed a little wooden, honesty tuck box by a yard but no cake there, just cans of pop and chocolate bars. Late in the morning I descended from the hills to Middleton-on-Tees. From above it looks grey and uninviting but would be voted by myself as one of the best large villages in England. There are a couple of cafes (I visited the excellent Teespot café), pubs, a hardware store, well-stocked co op, pharmacy and a few other shops lining the main street intermingled with old houses. The road is bordered by wide greens, trees and seats, the grass ablaze with the colour of crocuses, mini irises and snowdrops with daffodils waiting to follow. Everyone was friendly and there are lots of local walks. It really is a lovely place especially on a sunny day.

The Pennine Way follows the river Tees upstream through sheep fields and along old tracks. It was a gentle afternoon, I watched a couple of dippers and at one point came across a whole flock of oyster catchers rummaging about on a stony area of the river. There is an impressive waterfall at Low Force reached via a swing foot bridge. A few teenage boys plus their teachers were approaching me, the teachers presumably couldn't read as they all went on the bridge at the same time ignoring the warning sign of only one person at a time to cross! One lad was only wearing jeans and a tee-shirt but they greeted me cheerfully and said they were having a great time.

Further on is Holme Moss nature reserve and High Force waterfall surrounded by mature juniper bushes. A little later I passed a noisy quarry. I liked the fact that the quarry was there as part of the landscape, the ugly scar of the semi-eaten hillside across the river and on my side the wild land. We want and use aggregate. I met a couple wanting to know how far Cauldon Snout waterfall was, they had walked from Low Force and thought the sign said 2.5km but had already walked for several hours so realised it must have read 12.5km. They decided to return another day.

I had intended to camp at Langton Beck but couldn't find anywhere suitable. There were some lonely ruins across the river and a sign to the Youth Hostel. I did wonder if it was open but continued past Sayer Hill farm, where the manure pile was as high as the bedroom windows and entered open access land. I pitched my tent beside the river. It was a beautiful open spot with views along the river to snow covered fells but the wind picked up in the night and was buffeting the tent so much that I could not sleep. I ended up moving my tent into the shelter of an old barn at 3am. The sky was clear and full of stars, the ground solid. The morning was the coldest yet and I set off in the shade into a bitterly cold wind wearing two jackets with a scarf over my face. Once in the sun it was warmer but there was a cold headwind all day.

The river Tees pours out of Cow Green reservoir at Cauldon Snout via a very impressive waterfall. The Pennine Way scrambles up rocks beside it which might not be too difficult without a big pack. It was rather tricky and scary with the heavy pack on icy rocks, a hands, feet and knees scramble to the top where I discovered I could have ascended an easier way.

It is then over 8 miles of moorland to Dufton passing Birkdale Farm. I met the farmer and asked where his nearest neighbours were – 3.5 miles one way or 8 miles to the nearest farm in Dufton over the moor! It must be one of the remotest farms in England. The only sound was of gunfire from the neighbouring Warcop Training area which the Pennine Way skirts, or if you get confused, in my case enters; I hadn't looked at the map and so when red flags appeared to the left of the track having been on the right-hand side I thought I had entered the danger zone. I therefore set off on a vague track to the left over the moor heading for the river valley. Stopping after a while and looking at my map I discovered I had entered the range! Thankfully they were not firing at lone back-packers that day and I returned to the Pennine Way path unscathed.

It was very windy and open on the moors. I reached High Cup Scar, an impressive glacial valley which drops down to the Eden valley. It was even colder and windier along the edge but became more sheltered as I descended to Dufton. I half hoped Mary and Martha would be walking out to meet me and at one point thought they were. It turned out to be a party of walkers who sheltered against a rock face for a break. I arrived in Dufton alone by 1.30pm.

I like Dufton it has a mixture of houses, some very

old and farms with wide common greens. We had booked to stay in a 4-bed 'Hobbit hole' on the campsite for only £40. I texted Martha to see when they would arrive, they were three hours away. That gave me lots of time to relax, shower, wash some underwear and sort myself out before they arrived. It was good to hear they had had a good time in the Peak District with sunshine too and they gave me encouragement as to how much further north I was to when they left me in Horton. We wandered round the village, two young boys were playing football on one of the greens in shorts and tee-shirts, they breed them hardy in the north. We decided to go to the pub for dinner, an excellent idea as the food was very good and a reasonable price. I felt full on suet stag pie (it was the 'Stag Inn') and beautiful veg. It was nice having company as I was very aware that from then on I would be on my own. I was also nervous about going over Cross Fell the next day as it is the highest point of the Pennine Way. We were joined later by Josh, Mary's husband on his way home from a delivery job. The chef had gone home but the pub managed to provide a meal and then asked if we would mind moving into another room so that the local darts team could practise. For one awful moment I thought they wanted us to play darts, definitely not to be recommended with our throwing skills! For some strange reason as we left we were drawn into a conversation about woodland burials by the landlady, she was very enthusiastic about them, not that anyone was planning to die in the near future as far as we knew!

Chapter 12

Dufton to Kirk Yetholm; sun, wind & Hadrian's wall

9th-14th Sept.

The first day of this part of the Pennine Way over Cross Fell had been causing me some anxiety, the Cicerone guide ominously writes;

> "this is the longest and toughest day on the Pennine Way……these hills hold the English records for bad weather…..careful route finding is required on the initial ascent and over Cross Fell, where paths are vague…."

Cross Fell is 893m above sea level and is the highest summit in England outside of the Lake District, if it was an isolated peak instead of part of a great plateau it would be a mountain. Earlier in the week snow had been forecast but it was clear and sunny and thankfully the previous days winds had died down a bit, I felt much happier. After a good breakfast we said our goodbyes and I headed off to the hills whilst the others headed back to the island. From now on I was on my own on my walk.

On the narrow, stonewall lined lane out of Dufton I met a local lady with her dog, it was a large, handsome, brown, shaggy dog. She said it was a Griffon which sounded rather like a name from Lord of the Rings. She spoke about what a lovely village Dufton is and how advantageous it is being on the Pennine Way as it can support a Youth Hostel, pub and small shop. I asked whether there were many families there and was encouraged to hear that recent years had seen several babies being born and there were quite a few school children there.

My initial goal was Great Dun Fell, hard to miss with its massive 'golf balls' on top from which National Air Traffic services monitor aircraft as well as the weather. It was becoming increasingly windy as I climbed with gusts of at least 30mph but thankfully it was mostly a side/rear wind so hard work but manageable. I wouldn't have been able to walk there with the wind and cold of the previous day and I wondered if Blondine had made it over as she had planned. I did find what I think was her collapsible water bottle below the summit of Great Dun Fell but didn't see any footprints beyond so I wondered if she had turned back then. When I mentioned this to my family on the phone they joked she could have still been there somewhere, a rather morbid kind of joke.

It wasn't so far from there to the summit of Cross Fell. Tall cairns lead the way over the hillside and visibility was fine anyway. The summit is wide with a multi-sided shelter on top so it is possible to stand out of the wind, though there was deep snow in the least windy part of the shelter! I didn't linger long and soon headed down a boggy slope to get to Greg's hut bothy for lunch. It is a tiny, two room stone building with a stone roof, built at an elevation of 700m to house miners at the nearby lead mines. It would have been a harsh place to live and work but it provided a good shelter from the wind for lunch. Although the wind whistling outside sounded worse indoors and I noted the roof leaked badly. Since then the roof has been completely replaced, using stone tiles to retain the original character. A 'Pennine Way Girls' calendar adorns a wall; three local ladies in fun nude poses (a white towel providing modesty) at various points on the Pennine Way. I ate lunch reading entries in the bothy book; quite a few cyclists pass through as there are good tracks north and east, also mention of the Montane Spine race in January when ultra-runners attempt the entire Pennine Way in one continuous race! There was a LEJOG entry for October from three people, I couldn't imagine walking from Land's End to John O'Groats as a group of three, perhaps some had joined for just a while.

A long easy track leads down for miles to Garrigill which is an attractive village of stone houses around the village green, colourful with purple crocuses. Sadly the pub had closed down as I was thirsty from the wind blasting me. I made do with Lucozade from the tiny, old-fashioned shop. The Pennine Way then follows the river South Tyne to Alston through gentle fields. The route is shared with the 'mad as a brush cancer patient care walk river Tyne trail', recognising the therapeutic benefits of walking. I would agree with that idea from personal experience; walking was very much part of my recovery from breast cancer treatment in 2007. Following several months of chemotherapy and then radiotherapy walking was my road back to health, ultimately climbing Cader Idris at the end of the summer.

I had hoped to find somewhere to camp in Alston, having stocked up with food in the spar but the campsite was closed, the youth hostel had no room for tents and there were no suitable grassy areas. I walked back along the river and found a sheltered hollow in a field as it started to spit with rain. I had noticed cows earlier so checked they were not in the same field, I didn't fancy the thought of waking up to cows investigating the tent, it would probably end badly for the tent and myself.

The rain never materialised and my tent was dry in the morning. I ate with the door open, it felt like spring was arriving. I had passed a man with a great white beard the day before who had remarked that he was listening to spring in the trees, I could understand that, living in my tent close to nature. I walked down through Alston, it seemed rather run down with empty houses and the hardware shop up for sale. The steam railway and museum plus café were closed, the main attractions in Alston, perhaps it is better in the summer. I decided to follow the alternative Pennine Way route beside the old railway to avoid the innumerable stiles on the main route, I was tired of stiles. The day was mild with a weak sun, I removed my hat. It was peaceful with just the squeaking of lapwing tumbling acrobatically, their rounded wings appearing too large for the size of the bird. An old sign announced the crossing from Cumberland into Northumberland, I was in the last county in England! Earlier I realised I had at some point passed the half-way point on the Pennine Way but no sign acknowledges it, unlike on the Offa's Dyke. It was exciting to be approaching Hadrian's wall as I had never visited it and wondered if it would be a disappointment or be as impressive as I imagined.

Crossing moorland beyond the railway line I realised I could make out the line of Hadrian's wall still quite a few miles away. The Pennine Way takes a meandering route through fields in the Hartley Burn valley but then climbs up on to moorland through an 'interesting' farmyard at Greenriggs. I saw the PW sign and thought at first I needed to skirt round the wall through the fields missing out the house. But no, the Pennine Way goes through a gate and up a driveway, round the back of a house and out the back gate. All straight forward except for the old cars, couple of caravans and numerous hens and cockerels plus all manner of discarded paraphernalia in the way! Against the back of the house were four-foot high piles of very organised rubbish – bottles, cans and tins, enough to fill several skips. It was tragic to think someone lived there and might die there and not be discovered for weeks with people like myself walking by. I hoped they were still alive as I passed, the windows were obscured with dirty net curtains and there were no lights on, who could tell.

The Pennine Way frustratingly heads west once up on the moorland although ultimately you want to go east, there are no other paths to follow. Far to the west I could make out the estuary north of Carlisle and the sea, Scotland. Eventually I arrived at the village of Greenhead and went to the café for a pot of tea and food. Two ladies questioned me as to whether I was scared camping alone, something I had been asked before. I think news stories encourage this fear, I couldn't allow myself to be afraid else I couldn't have undertaken the walk. Also once in my tent I hoped people would presume it was a man camping. I know when I was in my tent by the Brecon canal a man had asked "are you alright, mate?" I had contemplated answering in a deep voice! They also wondered where I went to the toilet and how I had a shower, again something I had already been asked. I was hoping people didn't ask that because I smelt too much, perhaps I did, I hadn't had a shower since Dufton.

Greenhead is near a noisy road and I wanted to get to Hadrian's wall so I pushed on as far as Burnhead making it a twenty-mile day, but I felt good and the weather was excellent. I walked up to Hadrian's wall and was very impressed, it really is an amazing structure. The stones have all been cut to the same size and shape, a great contrast to the drystone walls I had been seeing. I spared a thought though for the thousands of slaves who built the wall, many had walked further than myself to get there.

I followed the wall all the next day rising up and down along the natural edge of the Sill, the Romans sensibly made use of the natural topography building the wall on top of a cliff. The wall can be seen for miles snaking across the land. At Housteads there is the remains of a great fort, now managed by English Heritage who charge £10 for the privilege of visiting it. I accidentally wandered into the museum section of the gift shop to be reprimanded as I didn't have a ticket! There was a cold, strong wind. I hunkered down outside below a wall to drink the take-away coffee I got from the machine inside. A man in Roman costume and lady headed off to the fort. It was amusing to watch day trippers struggling up from the car park to buy visitors' tickets, to then ask how to get to the wall, which is of course free to visit! One man, without a ticket walked through the gate into the fort then jumped down off the eight-foot high boundary wall and headed off beside another wall. It wasn't Hadrian's wall but just a wall built by 'Jack', some old farmer, probably using some of Hadrian's stones. I almost made the same mistake myself before I realised Hadrian's wall climbs up again giving excellent views down onto the fort. I hoped the man didn't think he was following Hadrian's wall.

At Sewing Shields (what a marvellous name) the wall becomes a mound with a ditch and runs beside a long straight B-road, or rather the road follows the wall. In the valley below I could see the 'Once Brewed' Youth hostel and the pub, Twice Brewed (more wonderful names). The names had intrigued me for years. As a young adult I had thought the hostel Once Brewed would be nice to stay at but now I thought the location by the busy road looked rather uninspiring. A large group of young people, including several from abroad, were sheltering by a lonely clump of trees eating. I presume they were heading to Housteads but it wasn't the most inspiring section of wall to walk.

I was no longer following the Pennine Way but a detour necessitated by storm damage in the Kielder forest. A couple of weeks earlier Pam had text me warning of the diversion mentioned on the Pennine Way website. Surprisingly there were no notices on the Pennine Way warning walkers of obstructions, except an earlier sign where the woodland was blocked near Crag Lough.

It was a long hard walk into a headwind beside the road and I was glad to turn north after Carrow and escape the wind. I headed through quiet valleys past isolated farms to drop down into the River North Tyne valley to Bellingham. It was another twenty plus miles that day, so much for not walking so far each day on the Pennine Way! In fact, on calculation, I had walked 62 miles in three days. It began to rain as I approached Bellingham, the first rain since walking to Horton with Martha nine days previously! I came to a camping and caravan club campsite before the town, it was open so I turned in to the site. For only £7.65 I had a sheltered pitch and use of a kitchen and large common room which no one else used that night – luxury. I even managed to wash and dry my hair as there was a hairdryer. It rained all evening so I enjoyed the novelty of relaxing indoors.

Bellingham is a lovely town with a good co op, butchers (where I bought three sausage rolls from the very jolly butcher) and a bakers who sell delicious scones and sly cake. My mum made sly cake, a name I always presumed she had made up, so I had to buy a slice of sly cake to see if it compared to hers. I decided that I preferred my mums as she used flaky pastry not the drier casing for the sugary currants. Bellingham also has a pharmacy, bookshop, post office, museum and train carriage café plus attractive stone buildings. It left me in a dilemma; should I vote it best small town or should Middleton-on-Tees keep the title? I decided they should share the title as joint best small towns in England. In retrospect I should also have spent two nights at the campsite and had a rest day. It would have been the perfect place to rest, sitting indoors eating cake and drinking tea.

It is big open country after Bellingham with far reaching views. The Pennine Way follows lesser paths and is boggier, this northern section is much less walked than the popular sections in the Peak District and Yorkshire Dales. Some areas do have stone slabs but they have sunk into the black bogs and who's to say how many Pennine Way walkers over the years have sunk down with them?

At the edge of the Kielder forest I again had to make a detour from the Pennine Way as the route to Byrness was obstructed by fallen trees. Martha had devised a diversion for me via Rochester further east, my destination for that night. The next day she had marked a route north via a Roman road to meet the Pennine Way where it exited the forest north of Cottonshopeburnfoot (just hope the locals have an abbreviation for the place!). I had to walk about half a mile along the main road to reach Rochester, the traffic was fast and passed very close to me. Rochester would have been a quiet place before the road became busy, old terraced houses one side of the road with their former toilets across the road. At the edge of the village is the Camien café, a sign proudly proclaiming that it is the last cafe in England. It looked rundown but I needed to fill my water bottle and fancied a cup of tea so I went in and found I had stepped back into the 1980's. A multi-patterned floral carpet covered the floor which looked like it had never been hoovered. An enormous chalk board behind the counter listed the many cooked items on offer. I settled for a pot of tea, it seemed the safest option, the cakes looking dubious being only one slice of each wrapped in cling film. There was only one other couple there in the large dining area. The café is up for sale, the owners looked ready for retirement. Another dining room led to the toilet upstairs, at one point there must have been accommodation too. At the bottom of the stairs was a cigarette dispenser, empty but with the sign 'not to be used by under 16's', hard to believe such things existed now. In the other room downstairs a glass cabinet displayed items for sale, a random selection of bleach, toilet paper, camping stove gas, gaiters, handmade jewellery and a single tin of sweetcorn and another of tuna! I dreaded to think how old the tins were but perhaps some passing walker would be grateful of them. I got the impression that the café at one time had been a busy place, now as I left it looked very forlorn with its numerous signs outside and a large empty carpark.

A little further on I turned off the road and up a track to the start of Martha's detour. I came to a gate with a big sign warning that I was entering the Otterburn Military ranges and not to pick anything up as it might explode! Martha's Roman road detour would take me directly through the firing range! Was she trying to get rid of me? I camped beside the river on the edge of the range where I could hear the noise of guns but hoped no stray bullets would reach me. Later I rang Martha to discuss what to do. I was only carrying the Cicerone guide to the Pennine Way and a section of map with the detour marked so could not see the larger area where I was. In support of Martha's detour the 1:50,000 OS map does not show the edge of the military range and marks the danger area as being further over, a rather serious error. It is also possible to walk through when the army is not active there, a public footpath is marked. The next day the army would be active from 9am to 5pm and so I needed another route north to the Cheviots. It also explained why on the Pennine Way website there was no alternative route for this section of the Pennine Way even though it wasn't possible to get through the Kielder forest. Studying the maps Martha said I could probably head north along a minor road from Cottonshopeburnfoot some five miles west of Rochester to then re-join the Pennine Way.

I set out at 7.30 the next morning noticing the red flag and warning light were showing. I had thought of perhaps setting out very early to get through the area before 9am but was glad I hadn't, thick cloud was obscuring the hills and I would probably have underestimated the time required. I began walking west along the road with the intention of hitching a lift. Thankfully there was a wide grass verge I could walk on. Several cars passed. Ironically they gave me a wider berth with my thumb stuck out than they did the day before when I was just walking! No one wanted to stop and I wished punctures on folk with bicycles on their roofs for not taking pity on a lone back-packer that Sunday morning. Then after about one and a half miles a van stopped and a lovely couple moved lots of things out of the way to allow me to jump in. They were both ultra- runners and were checking out parts of the Pennine Way before the wife ran the spine race in the summer. Her husband had already run the Montane spine race in January with three-foot snow drifts over Cross Fell, very impressive. The wife wanted to run north from Byrness to see if the forest was clear. The day before she had attempted to run south from Byrness to discover the Pennine Way utterly blocked by fallen trees. There were no warning signs until she got to the devastation, I was glad I had not attempted to go that way. They were happy to drop me off at the end of the road where a track would take me up on to the Pennine Way. Such kind people, they even asked if I'd had breakfast or needed any food or water, having a large supply of goodies in the van.

Heavy rain started as I set off and soon I was in thick mist setting off into the Cheviot Hills. It was like walking through a void. I saw signs for the firing zone which I was now to the north of and a sign giving a choice between continuing high up or a slightly longer hillier route via Chew Green and the Roman camp remains there. I had no intention of exploring Roman remains in the wind and rain so took the shorter route. The running lady caught me up and we chatted for a while before she went on ahead. I reached the Lamb Hill mountain refuge which looks like a garden shed incongruously anchored to the side of the hill. It is like a garden shed inside with the addition of a bench and minus any garden tools. I was out of the wind and rain though the wind sounded far worse inside.

The rain eased off as I left and the rest of the day was dry though the wind remained strong, giving a challenging walk. Windy Gyle certainly lived up to its name and I had to lean at an angle of 25degrees to make any headway. I met a couple of groups of walkers coming my way out for day walks, everyone looking very well wrapped up. Some feral goats were grazing the moorland. The views opened up revealing how extensive the Cheviot Hills are, so many hills continuing into Scotland. I could make out the three peaks of the Eildon Hills near Melrose which I would pass in a few days time.

I took the mile and a half detour to the Cheviot summit which I had climbed before in 1985 from the east. My memory was of a great, big boggy plateau with no real high point. It is still a great, big boggy plateau with a trig point on a large concrete base raised up above the eroded land around it. There are stone slabs forming a path but they have sunk by the trig point so it is a tricky bog hop to reach it. There were patches of snow around and no view from the summit. I was glad though that I had included it and quickly trotted back to where I had left my pack. I had been deciding whether I could make it to Kirk Yetholm that night but that would make a twenty-eight mile day and I was feeling rather wind battered and tired.

Reaching the Auchope shelter I stopped. The noise inside of the wind though made me wonder what sort of night I would experience, it is after all just a well anchored wooden hut. I only had some rather dubious water I had taken from a bog so I dropped down about one hundred feet to a stream. The stream emerges from the dramatic Hen Hole gully and I thought it would be nicer to camp down there by the stream. I filled my bottle and searched for a spot to camp. Trying a couple of places I gave up, it was too windy and the amount of flat ground very limited. It was 5pm so I told my-self to not be silly and to use the shelter, so climbed back up to the hut. It was fine inside with a good sized window and benches. I cooked dinner and read the entries in the bothy book. Some folk had also scratched their names in the wood panelling including dates of visit or short comments. I've seen this in other bothies, the bare wood bringing out the desire to deface something! Looking at the map later I discovered that the shelter is in Scotland, somewhere in the Cheviot Hills I had left England. I felt weary from the long days of the past week, I had covered ninety-seven miles in five days battling the wind, I needed a rest. The bench is quite narrow and I worried I might roll off it but I slept well despite the creaking and groaning of the roof in the wind. At some point during the night the wind must have died down as I awoke to silence. I lay there in the quiet and for a moment wondered if perhaps the roof had been blown off.

My last day on the Pennine Way was lovely, it was only seven miles, mostly downhill, to the end at Kirk Yetholm. I was glad I had kept those last few miles for the morning. The sun shone, the wind was behind me and the land covered in short grass, easy walking underfoot so I could admire the views. To the east I could see the North sea, I hadn't realised how close to the coast I was but then remembered when I cycled John O' Groats to Land's End I had seen the Cheviot Hills nearby as I headed down the A1. Meeting a road the Pennine Way joins St Cuthbert's Way and continues to Kirk Yetholm. It was mild in the valley, gorse was in flower and as I entered the village I saw gardens full of spring bulbs.

The Pennine Way ends (or starts) at the Border Hotel and outside a young couple were having their photo taken before setting off. They were walking the final section of the way to Hadrian's wall, it would be hard going for them into the wind and I asked if they knew about the closed Kielder forest section. They didn't so I gave them the relevant copied sections of the map and a brief description. Below the pub sign is an old plough adorned with lots of pairs of boots and trainers, many in good condition. It's puzzling to think people discard decent boots, either they have more money than sense or having walked the Pennine Way they vow never to walk again. It would be a good place to look for new boots! My boots were still in excellent condition after nearly eight hundred miles, they were staying firmly on my feet, they had farther to walk.

I went into the Border Hotel where you can sign the Pennine Way book. There was only one other entry for 2022, Becky 'the traveller' who came through one and a half weeks earlier. I felt as though I might cry or laugh with the relief and euphoria of completing the Pennine Way. Walkers, who have completed the entire route are offered a half pint of Pennine beer (evidently Alfred Wainwright had initially set up a fund for this). The beer was good, as were the burger and chips I ate for lunch, the first cooked meal since the equally good dinner in the pub in Dufton. I sat in the warmth making phone calls to share my completion of the Pennine Way with my family. I wanted to rest and just put my tent up, I was weary. I was happy too having walked the Pennine Way and had thoroughly enjoyed it; the scenery, not having to route find and the sense of achievement in completing a long distance route. I thought when can I walk it again?

Kirk Yetholm is great they allow walkers to camp there in the village on the green, perhaps it is a continuation of their history. A large stone memorial relates how a tribe of gypsies lived there in the seventeenth century and how their traditions continue. The lady in the pub said that in the summer months there can be up to ten tents on the green. I lay in my tent reading a book from the bus shelter 'library' as the rain came down and listened to the church clock chiming the hour and the quarter hours, there is no need for a watch in Kirk Yetholm. Edale felt a long way away, 267 miles to be precise, Kent even further, but I still had to walk up most of Scotland to get home.

Chapter 13

Kirk Yetholm to West Linton; drove roads & helpful folk

14th-18th March

I was trying to decide what to do. I had collected my parcel of maps from the Border Hotel but wasn't sure I wanted to follow my pre-planned route any more. My intention had been to walk through the Borders to the edge of Edinburgh, stay with a friend for a night then catch a train into Fife. I would then walk the coastal route to St Andrews where I spent four years at university in the early 1980's. From there I had planned to head North-West past Perth to Spean Bridge and then follow mountain tracks to Ullapool on the Cape Wrath trail. My friend wasn't able to see me though and I would be in St Andrews on the wrong day to run parkrun, which I had also planned to do. I was enjoying the peace and quiet of the hills and didn't relish the idea of Edinburgh or breaking off walking to catch a train. Nor did I want to walk through Edinburgh and over the Forth Bridge into Fife instead. I wasn't even sure I wanted to visit

St Andrews and see students in their somewhat surreal life. I needed to work out another route.

People had already asked me if I was walking the West Highland Way which heads north from Milngavie, near Glasgow to Fort William. I had walked the route in the first week of February 2017 and loved it; I would walk it again. I wouldn't need a map for the West Highland Way as it is well signed and I could remember a lot of the route. Once at Fort William I could meet my planned route near Spean Bridge. My route to Melrose in the Borders could be the same, I just needed to find a way to walk from there to Milngavie, which I was sure would be easy to find on the internet. I was worn out though and wanted a rest. I hadn't had a day off walking since the Wirral over three weeks previously. Hopefully I could find a campsite in Melrose where I could stay for a couple of days and use a library for researching a route.

I packed up the Cicerone Pennine Way guide and the map of Fife and posted them home from Town Yetholm's community shop. I bought a Selkirk Bannock there, a fruity bread/cake, it is heavy but so good to eat and I was near to Selkirk so it seemed appropriate. I ate breakfast in the Border Hotel before setting off; two sausages, black pudding, haggis and egg, more protein than I had eaten in a week. Only one other couple were there, they ate in silence, I wondered whether they were on holiday, they didn't seem very happy.

I followed St Cuthbert's Way for two days to Melrose, it was quiet with few people or cars around. I walked along footpaths and minor roads. On the aptly named Wide Open Hill, which is the half way point on St Cuthbert's way, I looked back at the Cheviot Hills in the haze and ahead to the Eildon Hills. In the distance I could see the Campsie Fells and Pentland Hills where I would be in a few days time. At the attractive village of Morebattle I stopped by the Kale water to wash and rinse out some underwear, it dried on the outside of my pack in a few hours in the sunshine and wind. The name Morebattle is nothing to do with wars, it is Anglian for lake dwelling –'mere botl'-as there was a large lake covering the wide valley which gradually silted up and then was drained. It is an area of fertile farmland with large ploughed fields but also areas of trees, especially old Scot's pines. Notices on fence strainers had been put up by a family looking for land on which to grow food and build a house or cabin. They wanted somewhere quiet and peaceful, one way of trying to find your 'dream'. At Cesspool there was a ruined house by a stream in a good size area of land. I wondered if they had enquired about that, though the name of the place would be a bit off-putting!

At Harestanes I followed the river Teviot through the estate past the gardens of the big house where walkers are requested to respect the privacy of the owners. The footpath was lined with daffodils and crocuses. Everything was closed at the Harestanes centre, which has local crafts, café and ice-cream parlour. I found an outside tap and someone told me it was good to camp in the neighbouring woods. A lady in her sixties walking her dog said how she loved to go off camping but hadn't for several years due to family commitments, she hoped to go this year. The woods turned out to not be good to camp in with too many old trees and not much space. When I found a possible site I could hear the barking of dogs from a nearby kennels. I carried on further and found a suitable corner of a meadow by Dere Street, the Roman road I had last met high up in the Cheviots. I listened to the loud barks of roe deer, which almost sounded like wild boar snorting. Initially I wondered what the noise was and was quite worried by the sound.

Dere Street looked uninteresting on the map being

straight but it is a lovely wide grassy track with old trees each side, another wild life corridor. I came to a plaque announcing Lady Lilliard's stone and the poem about her death in the battle of Ancrum moor in 1544

"Fair maiden Lilliard lies under this stane
Little was her statue but great her fame
On the English loons she laid many thumps
And when her legs were off she fought upon her stumps"

A bit gruesome and it may just be legend but I found it amusing. The poem was inscribed on an old unobtrusive metal plaque affixed to a rock. Next to it was a more modern board with illustrations, historical information and the poem. The board was going green and shabby as are all similar boards you come across in the countryside, many of them unreadable. I can't decide if I like such boards as I do find them interesting but wish they were more durable in the elements.

South of St Boswells I met the main road, St Cuthbert's Way veers off to take a circuitous route whereas Dere Street continues straight on. I did too, stopping first to don waterproof trousers as it was now raining. Half a mile short of St Boswells Dere Street spews walkers out on to the busy road, the woods and ancient route continue but there is no path and no possible way through the woodland. A few hundred metres further on though I could walk through community woodland to St Boswell Green, I think it would not take much effort to link it with Dere Street avoiding the main road. St Boswell Green is lovely with houses set back from the road beside large greens but it was ruined by the noise of the main road.

I re-joined St Cuthbert's Way and followed it down to the river Tweed which was wide with a strong current. When I met the road near Melrose I left the way which meanders over the Eildon Hills. They are probably lovely with good views but the clouds were covering the tops and it was raining hard. I road walked into the village of Melrose and ate lunch in a bus shelter, listening to three local women discussing the merits of the different butchers! Melrose is an attractive place but I was cold and wet, the abbey was closed, tourists were peering through the railings to see it. The library was closed too, it only opens briefly on two afternoons a week. Thankfully the museum was open, I went in and stood under the hot air heater waiting to speak to an assistant. She was most helpful when I asked where I might be able to use a computer and suggested I caught the bus to Galashiels, checking that the library there was open. A bus left in ten minutes from outside. I also noted that most people were wearing masks, I had got used to no masks in England but Scotland had always had stricter covid rules.

The internet is extremely useful for researching walking routes; I easily found descriptions of a way through the Borders via old drove roads and then over the Pentland Hills into the Central Belt. There I could pick up the John Muir Way which follows canals west all the way to the West Highland Way. It would be a simple and straightforward route and is in fact part of the Scottish National trail which runs from Kirk Yetholm to Cape Wrath in the far North West of Scotland. I had seen a sign on the Border Hotel indicating 470 miles to Cape Wrath. I also realised I could be home in just over three weeks. It wasn't that I was not enjoying walking but I had been away for a long time and wanted to see home, I was also feeling guilty being away so long. Three extra maps were needed to cover the route, I managed to buy two of them in Galashiels. The map covering Falkirk and the Central Belt though wasn't available, I would have to buy it later.

I caught the bus back to Melrose, it was raining hard,

I had been able to warm up and dry out in the library in Galashiels. Seeing that the campsite in Melrose was open I was hopeful that I could stay for a couple of nights to allow a day off before the next stage. I got off at the campsite, it didn't take tents until June and no they were full up and couldn't squeeze me in. I wandered down to the river and found a small patch of wet grass beside the path to camp. I was surprised to discover a frozen tent in the morning as I hadn't felt cold. Dog walkers and children enroute to school were surprised to find a tent by the river and some dogs barked in alarm.

I set off for Galashiels following the Southern Upland Way, first calling in at the bookshop in Melrose to see if they had the map, they didn't. It was a nice walk to Galashiels which was unexpected as from the bus the previous day everywhere had seemed very built up and busy, it was good to discover it wasn't. The route was for cyclists and walkers and there were quite a few of both. A bench at Tweedmouth station is in memory of Alistair Forbes 'still trainspotting', though not many trains pass as it is the end of the line. In Galashiels I posted home the sections of maps I no longer wanted to use, they had already had a tour of the country having initially been posted to my in-laws on the Wirral and then to Kirk Yetholm and now back home! Galashiels is a town of contrasting parts – 1970's housing estates and an ugly transport interchange then a grand town hall and big old stone houses.

Soon I was climbing up in to the hills enroute to Traquir. The Borderlands are very rural and empty, large rounded, tree covered hills and deep valleys. There is a strong sense of identity; in Melrose I had seen posters of sunflowers announcing Border children support the Ukraine, not I noted just Melrose children. In the pub in Kirk Yetholm they were discussing buying the Ukrainian flag to show their support for that country. Newspaper headlines were all about the ongoing crisis there.

It was sunny but there was still a cold wind and I didn't linger long at the three massive cairns on Three Brethren Hill. The three cairns are higher than a person and mark the border of three areas of land which explains why fences separate them all. In all directions the views are of forested hills. I passed the turn off to Broadmeadow youth hostel where we stayed once watching hundreds of bats emerge from the eaves at dusk. The area had been hit by storm Arwen earlier in the winter and there were large pockets of fallen trees in the plantations. Thankfully where trees had fallen onto the route it was possible to walk round on the heather. In the autumn the colour and scent of the heather must be wonderful.

Some sculptures have been added beside the Southern Upland Way; 'point of resolution' is circles cut in the heather to enable black grouse to feed. As you descend the hill by them though the circles change into ovals. At the edge of the forest I came across lots of slates with names and poems scratched on them, another art project. This had been to get people to list names of their horses in recognition of the importance of horses to Border people.

At Traquir the grass by the community hall looked very inviting to camp on but a 'no camping' notice was there. I continued past Traquir house, the oldest, continually occupied house in Scotland, to Innerleithen. I had hoped to camp by the river there but I found more 'no camping' signs and it was very windy with no shelter, so I went in search of the campsite. It was some way through the town, I was weary having again walked further than planned. It was open and for ten pound I got a sheltered spot and use of the toilet and water. Showers are an extra pound which I thought a bit much especially compared to the luxury I experienced at Bellingham. Innerleithen is a centre for mountain biking so a strange town as it didn't seem very wealthy but there are half a dozen expensive bike shops. In the Borders are the 'seven stanes' off-road cycling areas. I had come here with my son in 2013 so that he could explore on his bike while I went walking each day. It was a good trip during a heat wave, we stayed in bothies and swam in lochs.

It was another frosty night, I was pleased that I never woke up cold in my sleeping bag. Martha had also bought me some good waterproof gloves that I could wear when packing up my frozen tent which meant I did not suffer the agony of cold fingers in the morning. I probably should have stayed two nights at the campsite and had a rest but the weather was good and I wanted to keep going plus I hadn't really liked what I had seen of Innerleithen. It may be a lovely place but I didn't want to stay. An old railway line is now a tarmac cycle route to Peebles, it is a nice walk following the river Tweed. I saw some lambs and passed an apple orchard where there is the national collection of Scottish cultivars. I had a surprise at Cardrona which on my old map was marked as just a few houses but is now a large new village built around the time of the new millennium. I tried to decide whether I liked the mock estate style architecture of the houses or not. I noted a lack of chimneys and wondered how they managed in power cuts. Everyone was friendly and I realised that since entering the Borders people constantly said "enjoy your walk", an instruction I obeyed, I was enjoying my walk.

It was warm and sunny, I walked minus hat and coat. Peebles is as lovely as the name sounds, old buildings, colourful flowers and grass by the river, good shops, including an excellent bakers. I bought a coffee and donut to eat then and scones for later, it was difficult to decide what to buy there were a choice of five kinds! I crossed the road and, hesitating where to sit in the sun, was told that there was a seat just round the corner in the churchyard. I was sitting in the sun when the gardener came along and told me that the benches further on by the church had the best view in town over the river and hills. I said I was too comfy to move. A couple of minutes later a lady came along and told me the same thing! I finished my drink and thought I had better go and see the view. The view is lovely. The gardener was sorting out the border below, we chatted for a while. He was a walker and suggested where I might buy the map I needed and wished me well.

I bought the map for three pound second-hand in the bookshop, it was a relief as there was nowhere beyond Peebles to buy it before it was needed. I headed for Hamilton Hill where I could pick up an old drove road to West Linton. I was looking at my map to check which road I needed to take out of town when a mother pushing a buggy stopped to ask if I needed directions. As she began to tell me the way a man stopped to help too – people in Peebles are really the most helpful people in the whole country. The lady finished giving me directions and went on her way. I then listened to the same directions, with more details added, from the man. I listened politely as he was so keen to be of help and I didn't want to disappoint him and make him feel un-needed. At least it was not like the time I asked for directions in Barnsley many years ago when I was cycling; two ladies were telling me the way when a drunk man took my map and tried to help, I was afraid he was going to walk off with it.

I climbed up out of Peebles past the campsite, which was still closed. It looks a nice place to stay spread out on the hillside with trees and views. If it had been open I would have stayed and spent a day resting and exploring Peebles. I could have eaten more scones from the bakers, trying all the varieties. I arrived at a farm track with a sign indicating the old drove road to West Linton. It follows the side of Hamilton Hill which I am afraid to say is a rather non-descript, rounded, green hill. Sheep were grazing on the hill, one lay dead in the stream where she'd lost her footing on the wooden bridge. It was warm in the sun, I rolled up the legs of my trousers. I enjoyed the fact I was following another old way, this one would have been noisy and busy with cattle. Now it was quiet and empty the same as the other old ways throughout Britain. I passed some Highland cows lying lazily chewing the cud, they do not have to walk to market as their predecessors did.

I met two men out walking, the only people I met all day. They were leaving the forest, which was useful as I was concerned as to whether the route through the forest was blocked with fallen trees. The forest could have been gloomy but dappled sunlight came through the fir trees and further on the forest was more open with wide tracks. I exited the forest at a lovely stream which would have been good to camp beside but it was rather early to stop being only 2pm. In retrospect I probably should have stopped then and rested more but with the good weather and longer daylight I kept pushing on each day.

I found a camp spot before West Linton on the edge of an area planted with young trees. A stone wall offered protection from the wind. It was a lovely spot in the late afternoon sun which now set at 7pm, so different from the start of my walk when the sun set at 5pm. I watched the pinkish glow of a full moon rising, the actual moon obscured by clouds. My son text to let me know a lady my age who I gardened for had died suddenly. It was sad but made me glad I had taken this opportunity to walk as who knows what the future holds for each of us?

I ate breakfast with the tent door open so the rising sun

shone in, it was approaching the spring equinox so the sun rose just after 6.30am. There was the promise of a sunny day after another frosty start. Later it turned out quite hot, I could have worn shorts but they were not something I had packed back in January.

I came to West Linton, a lovely village with newer houses on the edge and the old houses and shops squeezed in beside the road in the middle, though there are rather too many cars for the narrow road. My route took me up a track towards a reservoir, it was quite busy early on a Saturday morning. I almost caught five women up who were on a circular walk from the village. They turned off the track up a hill. "Can you imagine yourself doing that?" I heard one of them remark, I presume in reference to myself.

The Lyne water below Beddingsgill farm looked very inviting in the sun but it was a bit early for a dip and I expected to find streams higher up in the hills. In the event the streams marked on my map were mere trickles covered with rush. I was walking up the Thieves' Road, an old drove road which takes you out of the Borders, over the Pentland Hills into the Central Belt via the Cauldstane Slap, the name of the pass between the two regions. I was about to start another section of my walk.

Chapter 14

Pentland Hills to Strathblane; canals and people
19th-21st March

I stood on the summit of Cauldstane Slap and stared, there before me was the vast, flat plain of the Central Belt with several towns and some great orange slag heap hills nearby. To the west I could see large areas of wind turbines and to the east the Forth road and rail bridges rose up. On the horizon I could make out the hazy line of the Campsie Fells with snowy mountain peaks behind. It was all a great contrast to the Borderlands behind me, I had completed another section of my walk.

An old Victorian sign erected by the Scottish Rights of Way Society Edinburgh instructs walkers to 'keep by the posts', before the right to roam open access laws. Another plaque informs that until the end of the 19th century the track was an old drove road. Later Victorian ladies walked that way taking the train from Edinburgh to West Linton and then walking over the hills to the station at Kirknewton, a fair distance. These Victorian ladies were quite undaunted. It was a very boggy descent to Harperrig and the main road, I wondered if the track had been a lot better.

Crossing the road I headed for the trig point on Corston Hill, except it moved, I was aiming for a sheep! The trig point was not white but a dull grey. The view was far reaching, I could clearly see Edinburgh with its castle and the towers and spires on Princes street with Arthur's Seat towering above. Beyond is the sea and Fife. Further west the supports of the new road bridge stand out like the sails of three sailing ships.

It was a bit unsettling to hear gun shots as I descended Corston Hill and to realise that I was above a shooting range. I began to have fears that a shooter would aim for the moving target silhouetted on the hillside instead of the stationary target on the range. It would be far more exciting for them. I tried to work out what I would do if a bullet came my way and where I would run to! I had definitely been walking alone too long. Reaching a minor road it was saddening to find the first lay-by covered with rubbish thrown from the cars and to follow a trail of litter all the way to East Calder. It was very hot and I was very thirsty, only having a flask of hot water left and I looked at all the empty discarded drink bottles taunting me. Perhaps I would come across a sealed bottle of juice which I could drink? I was feeling very fed up when I arrived at a house just before the railway. I could hear someone in the garden, the lady filled my water bottle and said how she often saw people walking this route to link up the Pennine Way and the West Highland Way. She had run a B&B so had had guests who were walking the entire country.

I felt refreshed and revived as I continued to East Calder where I decided to go in to the pub for a break and I also needed to recharge my phone. The sign declared that it was a village pub but it was more of a restaurant, busy with families. I ordered soup which came with a small piece of crusty toast and margarine. Now I like butter and couldn't remember if the menu said it came with a roll and butter but felt I couldn't ask. I began to feel frustrated with food not being what I hoped it would be like, I was missing cooking and having more control over food. I like butter and had carried the remains of a pack from Dufton, but had finished that long ago. Increasingly food occupied my thoughts, I would think of my favourite meals as I walked along. I could never feel entirely satisfied when I ate but also couldn't manage to eat much at any one time. It was a very large bowl of soup so good for rehydrating myself and I drank lots of water. Everyone was in summer clothes apart from a worryingly well wrapped up baby in a buggy, least I presume there was a baby somewhere beneath the pile of blankets!

East Calder is in an area of shale and at Broxburn there are plaques explaining that the Victorians mined for gas in the area. The vast orange slag heaps I had seen are a result of all the mining. I walked past one, Scotland's version of Ayers rock. They are the size of small hills with very steep sides yet motorbikes were being ridden up and down them despite the fact that large clumps of rocks fall from them. There are numerous 'danger' signs warning passers-by. It's quite a post-industrial area, the young cashier in the supermarket in Broxburn had asked why on earth was I walking through! There are though rows of attractive houses by the canal where the gas workers used to live.

I planned to camp by a ruined chapel near the canal at Winchburgh. On my map there were a few houses marked and nothing else. I discovered a very large new town development covering a lot of the blank area on my map! It seemed rather stark but there has been landscaping with trees planted and daffodils were flowering by the paths.

It just needs twenty years to mature and soften round the edges. The area is also quite noisy being near the M9 and under the flight path of Edinburgh airport but people need homes and I saw lots of families happily out walking.

I found a quiet corner of a field near the canal to camp, when I looked out at dusk several roe deer were grazing the winter wheat and I heard them 'coughing' in the night beside the tent.

I almost ran through the Central Belt along the canals. I knew I should slow down but I was anticipating the end and my mind and body kept propelling me towards it. The walk had become me. The days were long and sunny, I wanted to reach the West Highland Way in the sunshine which everyone said was going to break in a few days. I kept heading west towards the setting sun each day.

I was following canals, the way was flat though cruel on legs and feet as it is all tarmac. I had expected the more forgiving muddy surface of the other canals I had followed and I tried where possible to walk on the grass beside the path and not pace so fast, but the miles flew by. I regretted posting my trainers home, if I had thought about it, I could have posted them on ahead to Kirk Yetholm though I would be glad of boots if it rained.

I had been walking over twenty miles a day since Melrose and not had a day off. It was a serious error to have not programmed in rest days, every travel account I had read included days off. On short back-packing trips a rest day isn't needed but I had not rested since Sheffield. The first half of my walk had allowed time off visiting family and friends and although I hadn't always sat still I had rested from carrying a heavy pack for miles.

I was enjoying the walk immensely, seeing somewhere new, meeting people and just the simplicity of walking with the luxury of sunshine and a simple path. I had anticipated noise and traffic and lots of built-up areas in the Central Belt. I had only sped through it on the motorways or seen the land from train windows. Instead, as I walked along the Union canal I discovered how rural the area is, I watched roe deer heading back at sunrise to the woods which in a couple of months would be awash with bluebells. One morning, near the M80, sensing I was being watched I looked up and there about ten feet away was a roe deer standing in the misty reeds. Heron, swans, Canada geese and various ducks enjoyed the water and at one silted up area frogs were having an orgy amongst the reeds. A pair of bullfinch with their clean cut colours flew into the bushes. The birds were all in pairs, spring was definitely here.

It was a Sunday and yet again I was walking beside a canal; my first Sunday was beside the Lea valley canal, my fourth the Brecon canal and my fifth was the Llangollen canal through Trevor. The towpath was busy with cyclists, dog walkers and families. I could tell the time on my walk by the people who were out; early morning, throughout the country, I met the men dog walkers and runners. Later in the mornings the women dog walkers and cyclists and by mid-day the couples walking dogs and families would appear. The strong synthetic smell of fabric conditioner or perfumes wafted from many of the passing folk making me worried that they might be smelling me in my dirty clothes, I hoped not. I either didn't smell too bad or folk were polite as everyone was friendly and said hello and I walked short distances with people. I very much felt welcomed along the way. No one also showed surprise when I said how far I had walked or where I was headed, they meet other long-distance walkers. Two ladies told me of the man they had met the week before who was heading to John O'Groats, during the storms in England he had been taken in by a family for the week, sounded good.

I arrived at Linlithgow with its strange white star-shaped lightning conductor on the church tower. This evidently replaced the spire which was struck by lightning. Next door is the old ruined palace, it looked a nice town. I chatted to a local lady beside the larger-than life size statue of a cat called Dudley. It is in memory of the cat who had always loitered around the marina, I cannot ever remember seeing a statue of a cat on a plinth.

Near Falkirk is the high wall of the young offenders' prison and I could hear adolescent voices on the other side. It was sad to think of young boys locked up, only allowed out into a yard, is that really the solution to their behaviour? There is a large Tescos by the canal, I went in to shop which was just as well as the canals did not go past any other shops. It was a hot, sunny Sunday morning yet lots of people were going in with young children, I wondered if they really needed to go shopping in such glorious weather. At the permanent travellers' site next-door, several young children were out playing on electric vehicles, it seemed a lot healthier than shopping.

Before Falkirk there is a 630m long tunnel, the towpath continues through it and although there is a string of lights it does become very dark. People walking the other way emerged out of the gloom, their voices echoing against the damp walls. It seemed a long way in the wet before I emerged into the light again. I was looking forward to seeing the Falkirk wheel, the only other boat lift in Britain and the world's only rotating boat lift. It is an amazing piece of engineering though not really a wheel; built in 2002 it allows boats to go between the Forth and Clyde canal and the Union canal. The height difference is seventy-nine feet and previously there were eleven locks to negotiate. The canal had become disused and the wheel enabled the regeneration of the canals for tourism.

It was certainly a popular spot that Sunday afternoon, there also being a sponsored abseil about to take place. At first I thought it was bungee jumping as a photographic tent had that on their logo. I was slightly disappointed to not watch bungee jumping, probably because of a morbid fascination for it. Abseiling did seem much more sensible. The height is considerable but each abseil was over in less than a minute. On leaving I saw children playing by the canal and then the excited voice of one boy calling "he's fallen in, he's in the canal". I was relieved to see a soggy ten-year old climb out of the water, I am not sure what reception he got from his parents.

I thought of knocking on the door of an old lock keepers house to ask for water as a sign also announced eggs for sale. However as I crossed the lock I saw a young couple already there and when the door opened an old man emerged bent in half. He took them off to the hens and judging by the conversation was rather deaf so I decided not to ask, I may have just ended up with eggs. I was sometimes finding the strong accent hard to understand. A fisherman had told me all about his techniques with magnet fishing, I had nodded, not comprehending and wished him luck. I found another house by the motorway and knocked for water, the nice lady sent me to her outside tap and asked if there was anything else I needed. I was too polite to ask for a cup of tea and cake.

People in the Central Belt I have decided walk farther than elsewhere in Britain; normally I found places busier within a couple of miles of towns or car parks but near Kirkintilloch the canal was busy several miles out. I caught up with two ladies in their mid/late sixties walking to town. They live in Twechar and daily walk the five miles into town catching the bus back "the shopping weighs too much to carry home". They were lovely company and recommended the best place for coffee with excellent scones and where to go shopping for food. It was a shame I had never knocked on the door of someone like Catherine as she recounted how the previous summer a Danish girl had knocked for water. She had offered her tea and sandwiches and a shower. The girl said she did not need the latter as she had swum in the canal, we all agreed that would necessitate a shower! She had also visited the Isle of Lewis the previous summer, the highlight of the trip being a day out to St Kilda. It's a long boat trip and her friend had suddenly felt unwell and been sick over another passenger!

Later, near Lennoxtown, two men from Clydebank asked if there was another route they could cycle home not via Kirkintilloch. I looked on my map, there isn't. They were in their sixties, working class men in ordinary clothes out for a day cycling. When I worked out the mileage it was over forty miles. One of them sounded just like Billy Connolly, I could have listened to him for hours. The canals link up the whole of the Central Belt, the men had been able to cycle off-road from the river Clyde all the way to the Campsie Fells. It is also possible to cycle all the way from Glasgow to Edinburgh without using a road. I can certainly see the appeal of living in that area with so much easy access to the countryside as well as the cities. There was definitely a lot more appeal to it than living in the south east or the London area. In the Central Belt you are within sight of mountains and a short train ride takes you to Loch Lomond.

At Croy the John Muir Way, which I had been following, leaves the canal and heads uphill to the Antonine Wall, which I had never heard of. A larger-than life metal sculpture of a Roman soldier's head stands by the path. Antonine's wall replaced Hadrian's wall in AD 142 when the Romans pushed further North. My historical knowledge is so poor I hadn't realised that the Romans reached Scotland. An information board informs visitors that the wall was less substantial than Hadrian's wall being a four metre turf bank topped by a wooden palisade.

"Antoninus conquered the Britons a wall of turf being set up when the barbarians had been driven back"

was evidently written by an unknown Roman historian. The barbarians being the tribes north of the Campsie Fells. Not much of the mound remains but there is evidently the remains of a Roman fort on Croy Hill which sadly I didn't detour to as I heard later it was quite impressive. I met a dog walker from nearby Kilsyth who said what a great place it was for walking, to the one side the Campsie fells to the other the canal and a huge marsh where industry had been.

I stopped by the stream near Lennoxtown to paddle, my feet were aching and I had developed a blister below my right big toe from all the pummelling on hard surfaces. I applied some compeed. My shins also hurt from so much walking. Beyond Lennoxtown hills closed in on either side and the land became wilder with sheep grazing. A massive dog was lying prone on the path, its owners sitting on a bench beside it. I hurried up thinking the dog had collapsed but no it just lay like that on walks to rest! It must have weighed ten stone so could not have been carried.

An old railway line leads to Strathblane, I went in to the co op for food. I was walking on empty and still wanted to walk five miles up and over a hill to meet the West Highland Way that night. I added milk, water and three days of food to my pack, sat and ate some food straight away and then set off up the steep track in to the woods. A teenage boy passed on his bike to meet a couple of mates higher up, it was good to see them out enjoying their land. I was tired, my legs ached. I had walked over one hundred miles in five days from Melrose. On the stony descent to the West Highland

Way my left shin began hurting very badly. I stumbled down to meet the West Highland Way and camped by some very tall fir trees.

Chapter 15

West Highland Way; summer minus midges
22nd-26th March

It was nice to think that for the next five days I would be following a marked route and even though I didn't have a map it would be hard to get lost as the West Highland Way is well sign posted. The John Muir Way meets the West Highland Way three miles in but having walked from Kent it could count as starting from Milngavie. Perhaps Strathblane should be an alternative starting point for the West Highland Way. There's a great account by Hamish Brown of his walk with three friends along the West Highland Way. They refer to it as the 'Way Way'.

I had camped by the 'greenhuts' where post-war Glaswegians came to escape the city at weekends, they were similar to the Russian dachas I had seen when visiting there. The huts are now improved and most appeared to be permanent dwellings. One has a Tolkein theme called 'The Shire' constructed of dark stained wood with red painted window frames. In the porch are a selection of stuffed wild animals and a sign on the gate says 'haste ye back'.

It was not yet 8am but I met a man who had walked over

from Strathblane. He commented that I had set off early though he must have done so himself having walked five miles already. He asked where I had started and I explained that I had walked from Kent and he quizzed me to get his facts straight for when he recounted this to others!

A little further on a quiet stream made a convenient place to wash out underwear to dry on my pack. The day was already warm, it felt like summer. I delved into my pack to find a bandage for my shin which was quite painful and looked red and swollen. I began to have doubts about making it all the way to Ullapool, I would focus for the moment on reaching Fort William. I decided to go steady as the surfaces were still mainly hard, though up and down. I planned to stop at Balmaha for the night which is at the start of Loch Lomond, having camped there before when I walked the West Highland Way.

I enjoyed the walk to start with having forgotten how stunning the views of the Campsie Fells are. Last time I had remembered a tedious section of old railway line before the Beeches café but did not notice it now and was soon there. I was too early as the café did not open until 11am and similarly at the marvellously named 'Turnip the Beet', a zero-waste café growing veg outside in raised beds.

There is a section of road walking before Drymen. Four Glaswegian men were walking down the road near the campsite, one lingered behind asking

"Are you day one or day two?"

"Two months in" I replied and then explained that I had walked from Ramsgate in Kent, to which he uttered some expletive. When he caught up with his mates I heard him exclaiming this to them, I was feeling quite famous.

I followed the way up into forestry passing the hill my son said he had ridden up towards Loch Tay on his grand solo cycle tour of Scotland and England on finishing his exams at sixteen. A new sign indicates two choices for walkers; either via Conic Hill to Balmaha just under four and three quarter miles or via the B-road at two and a half miles. I opted for Conic Hill though later regretted my choice as the descent is extremely eroded. The path up was good and the views over Loch Lomond superb. It was very hazy so the wooded islands almost appeared to float in the water. It is a popular hill to climb, even on a Tuesday in March, I must have passed over fifty people ascending from Balmaha. It was a slow, tricky descent and I felt guilty contributing to the erosion.

Balmaha was busy with everyone enjoying the unseasonably warm weather. The village café sells delicious home-made ice-cream. I opted for raspberry ripple and vanilla and sat outside thinking that I could camp by 4pm and perhaps swim in the loch.

On entering the National Park there is a sign stating that you are entering a camping management zone from 1st March until 31st October. Camping during that period is only permitted on campsites or in the permit zone. A map marked four campsites before Rowardenen (though later I realised that one of those is on an island) but no mileage was indicated. However the man in the café said the nearest campsite was a thirty minute walk away, a bit further than I had planned but not too far.

I set off along the loch stopping to look at the statue of Tommy Weir, a great Scottish mountaineer. The beaches by the loch were busy with people but the path was quiet. I arrived at the nearest campsite, it was closed. From my memory I thought the next site was about another two miles so I plodded on, there was no possibility of camping by the path as it is all wooded. The path meanders through the trees, it's lovely but my leg hurt and I was tired. I reached the next campsite only to discover it was also closed. I could hear voices in the garden of the neighbouring house so went to the gate to be greeted by the sight of several voluptuous ladies in a hot tub. They were on holiday but said they had seen the warden around the campsite. I found him in a caravan and asked if I could camp. He said the site didn't open until April 1st. I pointed out that the National Park signs state you must camp on official sites after March 1st and that fines could be imposed, it was illogical that the sites were closed. The man suggested I continued two more miles to the forestry site which should be open.

I had no choice but to continue walking feeling annoyed that the private campsites and the National Park authorities were not co-ordinating. I know there are a lot of problems in the Loch Lomond area with wild camping and littering and people going to the toilet in inappropriate places but I began to feel that the National Park authority was to blame. The area is very accessible to Glasgow and people understandably want to come out and enjoy the stunning scenery and there is considerable pressure on the area, but the authorities are not providing enough infrastructure to meet these pressures. I had noticed that the visitors centre and toilets in Balmaha were still closed yet visitors are expected to pay for parking. I like wild empty places but feel that discreet toilets by Loch Lomond and opening campsites earlier in the season would solve some of the problems. I began to count how many steps it took to get to a particular point ahead, something I find myself doing when the going gets tough. Sometimes climbing a hill or on a long straight section of a walk I will look in front and choose a point which I think is one hundred steps away and count until I reach that point. It's probably not helpful but it keeps my mind focused and there is always the satisfaction of arriving at the chosen spot before one hundred steps! There is a recommended number of steps you should walk each day but as I walked I couldn't remember if a step is just one foot forward or if a 'right, left' counts as a step. Whichever I decided I definitely fulfilled the required number of steps.

The forestry campsite is unfenced and each camp spot is just marked by a numbered post with a larger grass area by the toilets. I reached the edge of the camping area and read the notice clearly stating that the site was open from March 1st and how it was legal to camp there after that date. I was therefore rather confused to reach the toilet block and see a large 'site closed' notice! However there was water and one of the compost toilets was unlocked, I was walking no further. I pitched my tent under the trees on the grass, the ground was shallow and hard but I had noticed the spots by the loch were just stony clearings. Two cars were parked nearby, their occupants were attempting to light fires on the beach. They were creating lots of smoke but no flames.

Earlier some fire engines had sped up the road, a wild fire was burning on the slopes of Ben Lomond above the youth hostel. It was some distance further on, I was safe where I was but Martha had text me concerned. In the summer we had seen a vast, out of control moor burn on the hills across the loch from where we live, it looked terrifying. Several years ago I was in the North West of Scotland with Mary back-packing when we saw smoke near the mountain Suilven. It was too far from a road to be tackled but by the evening it had spread towards the coast north of Lochinver threatening houses. We were staying in a bothy but at dusk the sight of the flames on the hillside nearby had us packing up and heading up the valley to camp by a large loch. Ironically the next day when we climbed a mountain and looked at the extent of the fire we had actually put ourselves nearer to the fire than if we had stayed in the bothy! We had felt safer though by a large loch.

As I cooked my dinner four Polish guys arrived, I had

passed them earlier sitting by the loch. They were also looking for somewhere to camp and were worried and confused by the contradictory signs. I said it was okay to camp but they continued further on.

It was beautiful walking along Loch Lomond the next day amongst so many trees. Thick moss covered the ground and large bilberry bushes grew under the trees. It was as well it wasn't late summer as I would not have walked far wanting to pick the berries, though there would also have been midges. With the sun and warmth it was summer minus the midges. My leg was also not hurting, I was enjoying myself.

Just before Rowardennen there is an old plaque on a wall

"A Request from the Holiday Fellowship.
Friend, when you stray or sit and take your ease
On moor, or fell or under spreading trees
Pray, leave no traces of your wayside meal
No paper bag, no scattered orange peel
Nor daily journal littered on the grass,
Others may view these with distaste and pass.
Let no one say and say it to your shame
That all was beauty here until you came"

Interesting words and rather dated but they got me thinking about the rubbish I had seen. I realised that one of the things I had seen all the way through Britain were dog pooh bags, left beside the paths or hanging in branches, or empty ones accidentally dropped. Infact on reflection I had followed a trail of dog pooh bags up the entire country, not a very pleasant thought. I started to rewrite the poem in my head, replacing paper bags, orange peel and journals with plastic bottles and dog pooh bags.

At Rowardennen I met the Polish guys again and an older English man, Richard, who had joined up with them.

He said they had camped in the permit zone, paying four pounds online for the permit but never getting a receipt or anyone checking them. The money solely pays for the privilege to camp on a small headland with no facilities! I had water and a toilet for free! He also said that he was hungry as he had not eaten since lunchtime the day before in Balmaha, he was planning to buy lunch at the Inversnaid hotel further north by the loch.

I left them and continued past the hostel and the few houses, outside one was an honesty box selling delicious 'Ben's Bakes'. I bought some biscuits and a very rich chocolate/sultana bar for later. Three fire engines were still attending the fire which thankfully had burnt uphill and not down to the houses. The ptarmigan track up Ben Lomond was closed.

It was a very enjoyable day, my leg wasn't hurting, the swelling had gone down overnight. The West Highland Way hugs the loch on a challenging path dropping down to stony beaches and climbing up again through woodland (unless you choose the alternative higher, flatter route to Inversnaid). It was beautiful with the warm sunshine, the loch hazy with perfect reflections of the Cobbler and surrounding mountains.

I stopped for a dip at a quiet beach, I had seen barely anyone so hoped no one would come along and be shocked. I shocked myself when I saw how thin I was. I had not looked in a mirror since Innerleithen and had not realised how much weight I had lost. I could audition for a certain genre film. The last week I had felt constantly hungry and food had never been far from my thoughts. I had tried to eat more but I had walked almost one thousand miles and my body just couldn't get enough calories. My last proper cooked meal was at the Border Hotel in Kirk Yetholm, that seemed a long time ago. My hip bones stood out and the base of my spine hurt on the hard ground at night. I felt mentally great but was worried that the walk may have pushed my body too far. I felt a little scared, the walk was taking over my mind and I knew I should have had a rest day. I glimpsed how the mind takes over in someone with an eating disorder, my mind was ignoring my body.

The cold water dip felt good, the loch is too shallow to swim near the edges and currents are dangerous further out. There is a memorial at one point to a young man who died whilst rescuing his friend who had got into difficulty in the loch. The Victorian sentiment on the plaque stating the great sacrifice he made for his friend, not sure how guilty his friend then felt for the rest of his life. I felt refreshed and clean. Later that day I stripped off again to wash my hair which dried quickly in the late afternoon sun.

I began to dream of a big meal at the Inversnaid hotel, I had enough food to get me to the next shop at Crainlarich but a proper cooked meal would be good. I couldn't decide if I wanted a burger and chips or fish and chips or jacket potato, the thought of such food creating imaginary tastes. I had not had a good meal for so long.

The two routes to Inversnaid meet near Rowchoish bothy which is an old stone building set among fir trees just off the track. I went to visit it and was surprised to find it bright and cheerful in the sunshine despite the surrounding trees. When I had visited it in February it had seemed a very dark, cold spot. It was good to see it otherwise. I met two men running and wondered if they were checking the route for the West Highland Way challenge at the end of May. Martha has run the whole route in twenty-six hours! I also overtook Richard and the Polish men having a rest, having taken the flatter route.

I crossed the bridge over the impressive waterfall to the hotel at Inversnaird; it was closed for renovation! I was disappointed to not get a good meal but sat and ate my own food until I saw the others approaching and Richard heading for the hotel door. I called out that it was closed and his face fell, he looked so weary. I asked whether he really had no food on him and he replied no, he had expected shops and hotels enroute! I offered him a couple of chocolate bars having nothing else to spare but he said he would be okay and would head for the shop at Beinglas campsite or the Drovers' Arms that night. The detailed guide book he was carrying marked them as only six miles away but I pointed out that the next couple of miles along the loch were the most challenging. There were now only three Polish men, sadly one had stayed behind at Rowardennen as his feet were blistered and so he couldn't continue (a fifth friend had dropped out on the first day).

I was dreading the next section of the path as I remember finding it very challenging but this time I really enjoyed it. In February I had been under pressure of time as it was getting late and being an overcast February afternoon it had seemed quite dismal. The way is a scramble up and down narrow rocky paths sometimes requiring the use of your hands. There are polished tree roots where hundreds of people have used them as handholds and the rocks under foot are worn and polished too. The route feels ancient and connects you to the land. The loch was mirror still, the sun warm, land reflected in water. Quiet except for the distant traffic noise from the road on the further shore.

I reached the flat grassy area by the loch where I had camped previously but continued over a hill to Doune Byre bothy. Looking into the bothy it seemed rather dismal but there was a selection of food in a metal chest. Taking a tin of sardines for myself I camped on a rise of rough grass nearby with a view of the bothy and ruined house next-door. A mound obscured the razor wire on the fence round the ruin! I could hear the gurgle of a stream and the bleat of the wild goats just visible on the hillside. During the night there was the sound of hooves passing the tent.

After about an hour the three Polish men came past followed by Richard who looked ready to drop down, he had not eaten for nearly twenty-seven hours, it was impressive he had walked so far. I told him there was food in the bothy and suggested that he should stop for the night which thankfully he did and he pitched nearby. The others continued. In the morning he thanked me for my advice and said he was going to walk to the Drovers Arms and have a rest day, I hope he completed the West Highland Way. He also had a summer tent with mesh lining so was suffering from the cold at night with the sub-zero temperatures. I felt guilty being so warm in my tent. A couple of other tents had appeared in the night, there were evidently quite a few walkers on the West Highland Way.

I had written in my diary that my left shin had not hurt at all that day and the only niggle was the blister under my right foot, if only it had remained that way......

Another cold start promised a dry sunny day, I set off marvelling at the views of mountains with snow on their summits. Hunger again in the night had me munching on slices of chorizo and chocolate. I was looking forward to stocking up in Crainlarich and perhaps buying a meal. The last section by Loch Lomond is beautiful with old trees and mountain views. That day there were lots of chaffinches too. I reached a closed Beinglas campsite then a stony track where my shin started hurting again. I bandaged it up and began seriously wondering if I could finish my walk, every step sent pain into the front of my shin. My route north of Fort William would be in lonely glens and on mountainous terrain. I would try to reach Fort William but today would concentrate on reaching Tyndrum.

A couple overtook me which confused me as I had seen them the day before at Rowardennen and presumed they were out walking for the day as she was carrying nothing and he just had a tiny rucksack. It took me a while to realise that they must be having their luggage transported! That seemed a good idea at that point in time though also a little bit like cheating. Coming across them having a break I asked about their luggage and they explained how they used to carry their packs but now they were older (they looked my age or younger) this was better. The whole organisation of accommodation and luggage transfer was left in the hands of the company but had not been without incidents; the previous night they had been booked into Ardlui Hotel where their luggage arrived safely. The hotel is accessed from the West Highland Way by the hotel ferry over the River Glas except it only operates after April 1st (that magic date again)! They could see the hotel across the water and rang them to be told to walk three miles to a bridge and then catch a bus back except on reaching the road it was a three hour wait for a bus! The hotel did pick them up and I presume deposited them back at the bridge the next day. Thankfully they saw the funny side to it all. There was something secure about carrying all your own stuff after all, even if the pack felt burdensome at times.

A little further on I caught up with the three Polish guys who had been allowed to camp in the closed Beinglas site and had walked the short distance to the Drovers' Arms for dinner. I walked a while with them and we ended up 'leap frogging' each other all day. They work in IT and so were finding the going hard on their feet, it was their first back-packing trip. They stopped every couple of miles when shoes and socks were removed and socks aired on their walking poles! One of them was carrying a tripod and camera to film their walk for friends back home, they wanted a photo of myself. I realise I never even learnt their names.

The section by the river Falloch is beautiful, the water so clear with many waterfalls. Then the West Highland Way dives under the railway in a hobbit tunnel, about 5 foot high so I almost had to crawl. There is a wide open valley above the road and railway to Crainlarich, snowy mountains and large plantations of firs and rough hillsides. The high voltage power lines are being removed and the lines laid underground so there were some bleak extra tracks and a lot of destruction. In a few years the valley will look a lot more natural. This section of the route seemed long and my leg hurt at every step, something was definitely not right.

I recognised the junction where there is the detour down to Crainlarich. It is marked by a seat at a view point by the forest, when I walked there before everywhere had been snow covered. The forestry has now been cleared and the track down was muddy and debris covered, I was glad to reach Crainlarich and see the shop. A sign outside advertised glass bottles of milk from the Isle of Gigha. I drank a 500ml bottle for lunch, it was delicious, just pasteurised milk with a thick cap of cream, not standardised or homogenised. It's a good shop with a hot drinks machine and microwave so you can heat up the pies which are for sale. Sitting at the picnic bench outside in the sun I chatted to a lady waiting for a train south. She had been walking with friends the day before in Kinlochleven which had been very hot situated as it is in a very narrow valley.

It is confusing as to how to re-join the main West Highland Way in Crainlarich. Walking through the village I arrived at a new main road with no signs to the Way. A workman suggested road walking two miles to where the West Highland Way crosses the road at Strath Fillian not something I wanted to do. A local then pointed out the route back up to where I had left the main West Highland Way. I caught up with a man from Ireland walking the West Highland Way, he was heading to Tyndrum too where he was meeting his wife. After a while I let him go on ahead at a faster pace than I could manage.

Strath Fillian is full of old ruins and there is an ancient burial yard. An information board has photos of ancient gravestones with interesting etchings on them. The stones are not visible though being covered with turf to protect them from the elements. I stopped at the campsite shop and bought an egg roll in an effort to eat more and also to rest my leg. Even getting to Tyndrum was becoming a struggle. The egg was runny so I managed to get yolk all down my front, I felt things were becoming 'undone'. I was very much enjoying walking the West Highland Way, it was a different experience to walking it before in February and seeing no one. It was in fact the first time on my whole walk that I met fellow back packers, apart from Blondine on the Pennine Way. I was though becoming increasingly worried about my leg and was concerned about what damage I was causing by continuing to walk. My body was tired out.

Approaching Tyndrum there are warning signs about mining vehicles using the track, a productive gold mine has started up there. In the past lead was mined there and one area of ground is still completely barren where the lead was processed. Now you can buy gold panning equipment in Tyndrum and try your luck in the river there. The next day I saw a man heading up river with equipment, not sure if he was successful. I was hoping the campsite would be open and so was pleased to see Pinetrees was and that they took tents. They only accept tents of walkers as the tent area is small but it was a lovely spot overlooking the stream. Later the Polish guys joined me.

I rang home to discuss what to do about my leg, Martha

suggested I rested up for a day or two to see if my leg improved. She didn't want me to stop and then regret the decision. We thought it could perhaps be shin splints. I walked to the nearby 'Good Food café' for dinner and met most of the walkers I had seen that day. I ordered the Hebridean trio- battered sausage, haggis and Stornoway black pudding with chips. It was a struggle to finish it all, it was so long since I had eaten so much in one go.

I spent a long time enjoying the hot shower, my first since Dufton and inspected my left shin. It was red and swollen at the front, I did not think I could walk any more but had optimistically restocked with food and hoped it might improve with a day of rest. The swelling did go down overnight and I wished the Polish guys well as they set off for Kingshouse, the next day. They would have lovely sunshine to walk over Rannoch moor. I walked slowly to the 'Green Wellie' services to buy a book. By the time I returned to my tent my leg was swollen and I could barely walk. I lay down by the stream in the sun and read all day. My leg did not improve. Later I rang home, Martha had looked up about shin splints and saw that they can progress to a stress fracture and agreed that it was silly to continue. I could return in the autumn and complete the walk.

Several tents had joined me in the night including one which looked very much like one of the Polish guys. Packing up my frosty tent for the last time I saw him outside his tent but I couldn't stop as I needed to catch the bus. I wondered what had happened and whether he had turned back from a cold high up camp at Kingshouse.

Feeling sad for him as he had made it half way I dropped the toilet block key off at the reception and hobbled to the bus stop. It was time to go home.

Chapter 16

West Highland Way part two; autumn colours
19th-25th Oct

Towards the end of October I at last set off to finish my walk after a frustrating summer. Initially I was more exhausted than I had realised and so it was good to rest, eat and begin writing this book. I had a tibial stress fracture, the cure for which is rest and pottering around. Pottering was all I was capable of doing, I couldn't even walk to the end of our drive and when my neighbour invited me over my son had to carry me there! After a while though it got frustrating not being able to walk very well or run and there was lots needing to be done here in preparation for the growing season.

By the end of May I was fully mobile again but then developed achilles tendonitis so more rest and strengthening exercises. Sometimes it felt that the walk had broken my body but I did not for one moment regret undertaking the challenge and wanted to complete it. On reflection the injury was partly my own fault, I had failed to take days off at the end of the walk. My mind was focused on the walk, resting isn't something that comes easily to me.

In the meantime national events had taken place; we now had Liz Truss as prime minister and the queen had died. On a personal note my friend John, who I had lunch with in the Forest of Dean, had died a few months after being diagnosed with cancer, sadly in hospital and not at home with his beloved view of the river. Again it made me glad that I had undertaken the walk and caught up with so many friends. The situation in the Ukraine had been pushed into the background as the royal family took president in the headlines. Sarah's married daughter, who had remained in Russia, had crossed through the chaos of the Georgian border with her husband so that he could escape the enforced conscription. Covid-19 was making headlines again as yet another variant was appearing, but travel was allowed, it was time to set off again.

It took most of the day to return to Tyndrum so there was only an hours daylight left when I got off the coach. I did contemplate going to the campsite, which in the interim had changed its name to Tyndrum Holiday Park, but I wanted to enjoy my tent alone so set off up the West Highland Way. Finding a sheltered area of grass by the track a few miles away I set up camp. While cooking dinner I could hear cows lowing and remembered that there were cows in that area before, not that I had seen any signs of them this time. I put on my headtorch and set out in the dark to investigate and a bit further along saw lots of glowing eyes looking at me. It was fine they were the other side of a firmly shut gate, I wasn't going to be trampled to death as I slept. I would have to face walking past them the next day but could deal with that problem in the morning.

The next day I set out at first light, about 7.30am. That was ironic as I had planned to have lots of daylight when walking this section, not to be walking into shorter days. The cows thankfully had vanished and it was a lovely walk to Bridge of Orchy. The autumn colours were stunning especially as the trees back home had already shed their leaves. The route follows the railway line and before long crossed it, there is a three ton weight limit on the bridge. I think I was well below it even if my pack was feeling heavy. The Caledonian sleeper went past enroute to Fort William. Bridge of Orchy is a handful of houses and a hotel by the river. I was surprised to see quite a few West Highland Way walkers, some still packing down tents and others photographing the bridge. I thought it was a bit late in the year to meet many people.

The route climbs through felled forestry then a rough track descends to Inveroran which has a hotel (closed at that time) and some estate workers houses. It is attractive there as there are quite a few trees as well as meadows by the river. A cobbled track, courtesy of Telford, leads up on to the edge of Rannoch moor. I stopped by a stream to have a rest and some food. I was trying to take the walk steadier. Two women came along who were from Norfolk and taking eight days to walk the West Highland Way staying indoors, it sounded nice. We chatted for a while and I discovered that Catherine had been following my walk on facebook! They carried on, Catherine to find more waterfalls and her friend to look for mushrooms, they were very much liking the change from Norfolk landscapes.

It started to rain and so I crossed Rannoch moor in low cloud and wet which was a shame as it is a wild and beautiful place. It rained the first time I walked across the moor from Corrour station in 2012. Low clouds do give the moor a great atmosphere, reminiscent of Robert Louis Stevenson's description in 'Kidnapped'. I had been given the book as a twelve year old and found it very inspiring, reading for the first time about Scotland and to me inconceivable landscapes.

Reaching the Glencoe Mountain centre I headed for the café to dry off. It is a strange centre half way up a mountain-side overlooking the moor. There is a dystopian feel to it, not helped by the extremely large car park with a double row of wooden pods (deluxe cabins I think is the description given in the advertisement) facing it. Beyond the café a chair lift disappeared in to the clouds, the empty chairs ascending and equally empty chairs returning. I wasn't sure why it was actually working, everything felt very weird. The café was lovely, airy but warm and excellent food. Lingering over a very cheesy jacket potato and copious amounts of tea, I stayed for a while along with quite a few other walkers and cyclists hiding from the rain.

Eventually I forced myself to put my wet waterproofs back on and continue. I followed the road down to the Kingshouse Hotel with its new extension and bunkhouse. I had wondered about camping there but it all looked very wet and any campspot would have been lit up by the hotel lights, so I continued. An Australian couple were photographing the iconic view of the bridge and Buachille Etive Mor, except there wasn't a view. Then I caught up with three eastern European guys walking the West Highland Way, one wearing a blue tartan kilt and all looking very wet in trainers. They were aiming for Kinlochleven that night which was another eight miles over a mountain. I found a grassy area by a stream to set up camp. It was above the A82 but the gurgle of the stream cut out any traffic noise and there was something quite satisfying about looking at the vehicles passing from the comfort of my tent. Across the road was Buachive Etive Mor, the mountain which features on so many calendars and postcards, except it was invisible that day.

The night before when I had put up my tent one of my walking poles had refused to stay up which had not been a problem as the other obliged. My tent needs a fully extended pole to function as it does not have its own tent poles. Now the other walking pole had also gone on strike, what to do when I was on the side of a mountain in the rain and it was going to get dark soon? I managed to improvise by cutting a hair twiddle and tying it securely round the pole but I did think it ironic that my equipment was giving up on me this time. I had also discovered that the screen on my digital camera no longer showed anything so I was taking photos 'blind' hoping that the camera still worked. The camera did date back to 2007 so I suppose it had lasted a long time.

I found a text from Pam to let me know that the prime minister, Liz Truss had resigned. She had only managed a couple of months. I was not only going to finish my walk with a King on the throne but a different prime minister. What else was going to change?

In the morning the rain had stopped and the clouds were lifting giving brief glimpses of the mountain tops and crags. It was all very atmospheric. I set off up the 'Devil's staircase' which is rather a misnomer as the climb isn't that bad and you soon reach high ground with wonderful views of mountains. The descent to Kinlochleven is far longer especially as you can see the houses several hours before reaching the valley. A few groups of people were walking up. The view down to the houses feels almost Alpine. The sun was shining in the village, during the winter months the sun does not reach the deep valley. I went in to the co op and bought a banana and sat in the sun to eat before crossing the bridge to Kinlochmore, the two places are almost joined. The West Highland Way heads back uphill through woodland. I was surprised to come across the three guys from the night before just packing up their tents as it was now mid-day. They had not arrived until 8pm the night before and obviously had no plans to set out early, but they had left their campsite late the day before too. Perhaps they liked walking in the dark and they made their camps very comfortable with music playing and clothes hanging up to air.

It became very warm as I climbed up through the mixed woodland and apart from a mother and child, coming down to the village, I saw no one. I find it strange how memory works as I had no recollection of the long empty valley that the route goes through before Fort William. I could see the path climbing ahead through the valley past a couple of ruined houses but there were no West Highland Way markers for miles. I began to wonder if somehow I had missed a turn off and was heading the wrong way. I did though recognise the route when it entered some forestry and a minor road turned off. When Martha and I had walked it before there was a diversion down this road to Fort William as the forestry had been blown down by a storm. The forestry now has been partly cleared and some sections are birch trees.

I wanted to reach Fort William that day and remembered that when we had walked from roughly the same camp-spot we had arrived in Fort William mid- afternoon in time for Martha to catch a train. I naively thought it would not be that far to the Fort, not realising how much shorter the diversion we had taken was. The forest route is very long and took far longer than I expected. I enjoyed the views of a snow topped Ben Nevis but was wishing for there not to be so many twists and turns and ups and downs on the path. I came across an older man and his daughter resting on a rock, they were also heading to Fort William that day and were finding this section long. I was very glad to eventually reach the campsite as the daylight was fading. I had passed a good camp spot just before the forestry and regretted not camping there as I realised I had yet again walked over twenty miles.

Another three eastern European men were in front of me to book into the campsite (they always seem to come in threes). The lady asked them if they had walked the West Highland Way and questioned them about it. She didn't ask me, which made me feel ignored. She was actually quite sharp with me as I couldn't remember my phone number and said I should know it. I felt like pointing out that it would be pointless ringing me as I had switched off my phone and surely if they found me collapsed in my tent they would not ring me! The lady in the camp shop on the other hand was lovely and found a selection of abandoned walking poles for me to choose one for my tent that night.

It's a good spacious campsite with different areas to choose from, each with a name – 'Hill side, 'Ben view', 'Deer park', the latter slightly dubious giving thoughts of the possibility of ticks. I bought a can of Loch Lomond beer to celebrate completing the West Highland Way, it was good to be back on my walk.

I left the next morning in the dark, torches shone on the path ascending the Ben. It was a mild, still morning, and was a while before the birds started to sing. I wanted to arrive in Fort William in time to go shopping before catching the little ferry across to Camusnagaul over the loch for the start of the Cape Wrath Trail. It was barely light when I arrived in town as it was a quicker walk than I thought. The selfie photo I took with the statue of the walker resting his feet on the bench marking the end of the West Highland Way looks as though it was taken at night. I went to the large Morrisons to stock up on food for several days and then went on a walking pole search. There are quite a few outdoor shops in Fort William but I needed poles that extend to 140cm which quite a few models don't. I was also surprised to find some poles gender orientated, with shorter ones for ladies. What about tall ladies or short men? Eventually I bought a pair in the first shop I had visited and so went to find the ferry. Later I read the instruction information for the poles warning to use them correctly and inspect them regularly 'failure to follow these warnings may result in catastrophic failure of the trekking poles, causing serious injury or death'! Serious stuff these walking poles, my old ones had catastrophically failed as regards to putting up the tent but hopefully deaths caused by failed walking poles are few and far between. Though if they do occur you have been warned!

The ferry is a tiny boat and only takes five minutes to cross the loch. I was quite disappointed it didn't take longer as I rather enjoyed the low view of the water and the different mode of travel. I was the sole passenger but there were three women on the other side waiting to come shopping in the Fort. It does save a long drive round and is also promoted as a cycling route as the road once across is very quiet. I had to walk south along the road for about six miles and I think only half a dozen vehicles passed me the whole time. There were a few houses at the start, one weirdly has a life size model of a gorilla in the front garden! Beyond the houses the road wandered through mixed woodland loosely following Loch Eil.

I tried to walk at a slow pace and not think about the end goal. I focused on the details around me – the moss on rocks, curlew and oyster catchers on the shore, the colours of the leaves. At Inverscaddle Bay I stopped for a break watching the sheep grazing on the saltmarsh. I wonder what makes a sheep stop grazing one area and walk through water to reach another area which looks identical? As I started up the road by Conaglen house a red squirrel ran into the trees.

I walked up Cona Glen which is beautiful, the autumn colours were superb and at the start are towering giant redwoods and gnarly old oak trees. I stopped by a side stream for a dip, the water crystal clear and refreshingly cold.

Higher up, the glen is more open with remains of the old Caledonian forest on the hillside. Some areas are fenced off and have been replanted. Half way up is an attractive bothy at Corriarich, I stopped for a rest and felt a bit disappointed that it was locked. I had also thought I was much further up the glen. Eventually I camped at the head of the glen where I could see the next days path climbing up. I was by the stream and there was a small beach. I sat in the late sun watching a group of deer warily crossing the stream. I was upwind to them but they sensed something wasn't quite right. Dinner was eaten in the tent as the temperature plummeted at dusk but I was enjoying being in the wild, camping again, a long way from any road. I felt weary but so far nothing was hurting. I thought perhaps I would try to walk less far the next day having had two long days.

It was trying to rain in the morning and the clouds were down, I put on full waterproofs and set off out of Cona Glen. The path is an old grassy track and the climb was easy but the descent was eroded and stony. Somehow I twisted my right ankle and ended up on the ground. I have sprained my ankle a few times over the years, initially I was more annoyed that I had torn the knee of my waterproof trousers. I stood up, my ankle didn't hurt to walk so I carried on.

The rain never materialised and the clouds cleared. Looking down towards Glenfinnan valley there was a temperature inversion so the valley was full of clouds, it looked very beautiful. I entered woodland of great old Scots pines and came to a stream. Removing my boots I waded across as I didn't want to get water in my boots which were dry. The track was good to reach the valley, I then had to walk nearly two miles along the road to reach Glenfinnan as a bridge further along was broken. I am familiar with this road to Glenfinnan as I once walked the eighteen miles from Lochailort to Glen Ffionligh (beyond Glenfinnan) along the road. It had not been intentional but I was at the start of the TGO challenge and having attempted to enter the Knoydart had been turned back by the full rivers. I then walked the road to get back on my route. I did contemplate hitching then but the TGO is supposed to be a walking challenge from coast to coast. It was only later that I learnt I had set out in the end of a hurricane and that a lot of the other walkers on the challenge had stayed put all day.

The Glenfinnan visitors' centre car park was busy with cars and coaches. I bought a coffee and pastry and took it to the seats outside. An opportunistic robin came and sat on my table demanding food. I gave it some pastry. A coach party of folk from the Central Belt came back from viewing the viaduct, one man happy to have seen the steam train go past. Some of them tottered down to see the memorial by the loch but most came to the café.

I crossed over the road bridge to take the road up to Corryhully bothy, it's flattish and tarmac. The tourists dutifully follow the signs over rougher ground to the viaduct, famous for featuring in a Harry Potter film. I even saw a few people in Hogwarts scarves. I presume there is an invisible forcefield at the viaduct which most do not dare to cross as I only saw three people walking beyond it. The walk up to Corryhully bothy is so easy and gives you glimpses of wonderfully rugged mountains as well as following the river Finnan, it is sad people do not venture so far. The bothy is a low stone building beside some old fir trees. Martha, Mary and myself came here one easter when there was snow on the ground and were welcomed by the estate keeper who provided wood for the fire and even lit it for us!

The track continues beyond reaching a bridge which I was relieved to see is a substantial wooden bridge with handrails. That easter we had had to cross on two parallel metal girders and not think of the raging water below as the rivers were in spate. I followed the track up Gleann Cuirneen which is a lovely pleasant climb on an old grassy track. Again it was different from my previous experience when we had descended the track in the rain and discovered a recent landslide. To be safe we had traversed the landslide separately in case more rocks had fallen, now I could barely discern where it had happened.

At the top of the pass there is a gate in the middle of nowhere with a sign attached 'please shut the gate'! The gate was closed, there is no fence. Three people plus a dog had over taken me on the ascent and just down beyond the gate I met them having a break, their food spread out on a cloth on top of a large rock

"Would you like a drink and food" they asked.

"No thank you" I said politely then thought wait, what am I doing turning down food when walking?

"No, yes please, can I have a banana?"

This was definitely a first on my trip, or any trip, being given hot chocolate (they had their camping stove out) and food in the mountains. I could have eaten more but didn't want to appear greedy and definitely did not want the offered kiwi fruit. Who brings kiwi fruit out on a walk? We chatted for a while, they came from the Mallaig area and belong to a training group and try to come out for weekly walks. They had thought to walk down to Loch Arkaig but were concerned there wasn't enough daylight so were going to turn back. I didn't feel guilty eating their food, they would be back home that night. I asked one lady if she could take a photo and email me it in case my camera was dead. When I gave my email address she said she thought I would be called Jane!

The descent to the valley was very slow, initially because the path was rather steep but then it was due to jumping and dodging all the bogs. The views were lovely but the land not easy, it is an extremely wet valley. We had walked up it before in heavy rain but it seemed no drier this time. Near the bottom I met a track and then came to a ford so off with my boots. I was shocked to see the state of my ankle, it was swollen and the skin red half way up my calf. Oh well I thought the cold water would be beneficial to the swelling. I sat on a rock to replace my socks and boots then walked over the brow of the hill to discover the track recrossed the river! In total there are three fords to negotiate before reaching a bridge to enter the forest.

I was glad to reach the forest and an easy forestry track to follow to the bothy at A'Chuil. I had thought of not going so far but there was nowhere to camp in the valley as it was too wet and nowhere in the forest. I was also hoping that perhaps there would be company in the bothy. There was company, but not of the kind I wanted, it was the rather small, noisy, annoying kind. As soon as I switched my headlight off the mice had emerged, initially gnawing at an empty food packet which someone previous had left in the hearth. I had hung all my food up as a precaution. After a while I decided to give them a large dollop of peanut butter as there was a jar left in the bothy and I hoped if they had enough to eat they would be quiet. It had worked once before in a bothy, we had given the mouse a digestive biscuit and it had eaten its fill and been quiet. I awoke later to a wooden, banging noise, a tiny mouse was carrying the plastic spork in its mouth across the wooden floor and proceeded to try to squeeze it through a narrow crack in the doorframe! I did not sleep well as there were also car lights from the lodge across the valley shining through the window, in addition to listening out for the mice in case they tried to eat my possessions.

I awoke feeling tired and generally rotten. I inspected

my leg which I had diligently kept raised all evening. It did not look good, there was swelling and discolouration half way up my calf and my foot and ankle were badly swollen. It felt like a deja vue. I obviously could not continue my planned route. I had intended to walk into the Knoydart and through to Shiel Bridge, a journey of three days. If I walked that route I would probably end up calling mountain rescue, I needed to go another way.

I tried walking around. Strangely my ankle did not hurt to walk as long as I was careful how I placed my foot. I decided I would try to hobble back along the forestry track and out to the road end at Loch Arkaig. I didn't have the loch on my map but knew that if I walked along the road I would eventually reach the Great Glen. I didn't want to go home yet, I had only walked four days and it had cost time and money to get to Tyndrum, perhaps I could walk up the Great Glen Way to Inverness. I was hoping also I could hitch along the road. If I couldn't manage to walk out there was a light on in the lodge over the river. I would hobble down to the river and cross to ask for help at the lodge, hoping that the broken bridge there wasn't as bad as described in the bothy log book.

It was annoying that I was injured again, the end of my walk seemed fated. In some ways I hadn't fully prepared for the return to the walk; we had been busy with the roof being replaced which had not been without problems. My leg had required five stitches from an encounter with a slate and I had left with the end of a bad cold and cough still lingering. I had also been over enthusiastic in my calculations of how long the rest of the walk would take me, I should have allowed shorter daily mileages.

Packing up I left in the half light, watching a bat flitting around. Stags were roaring, I heard them in the night too. I walked slowly along the track enjoying the walk, I couldn't hurry and was resigned to not getting to the end of my planned walk again. I reached the road, a lone car was parked up, presumably someone had left it to go off walking. I had passed a house which appeared empty so only the lodge gave the possibility of a lift. I set off along the road which meanders beside the loch. I decided to go slowly and just enjoy it, low ribbons of clouds hung above the loch and across the water Scots pines were silhouetted against the sky. It was all very beautiful.

A couple of miles along the loch is the first house, Murlaggan, it was locked up. There were lots of trees around and birds; thrushes, robin, tree creeper and sparrows and some noisy birds I couldn't quite see (later I identified them as crossbills by their sound). A sea eagle flew across the loch. I then saw a campervan parked overlooking the loch, so that made another possibility of a lift.

I stopped for a break and marvelled at the different colours of the autumn leaves. Loch Arkaig has lots of native trees lining the valley. I heard a vehicle, an oil tanker passed going up the valley. There was now some hope of a lift as it would have to come back down the loch after delivering oil.

Loch Arkaig is very long and I wondered when I would reach houses, trying to remember how long the loch is from looking at maps. There is a sign for a butterfly reserve in some woodland, not what I expected to see. A car was parked by the road, below in the trees by the loch a man and his dog had an established camp. I wondered if he lived there permanently. I came to an area of private, numbered plots by the loch, some had old sheds, caravans and outside sinks. I passed a house but that was all, there was a distinct lack of people.

I was feeling weary as although my leg didn't hurt it was tiring to walk. Then I heard the sound of the oil tanker returning, would he stop and give me a lift? He did, it was a long way up to climb into the cab and a quick ride to the end of the loch and the Great Glen. I jumped out at Clunes where I saw a Great Glen Way sign.

Walking down to Loch Lochy I pitched my tent by the shore, it was only 2.30pm but I wasn't going any further. I didn't feel that well but decided I was probably dehydrated so had some tea then fell asleep. Later I awoke and lay listening to the sound of gentle waves on the loch and the gurgling of a small stream. I thought about what I should do, whether to just head home or to try walking the Great Glen Way. I had planned to walk the route one January but then covid happened so I decided I would give it a try now. If I couldn't walk I would easily be able to reach a road and get myself to Inverness and home. Having decided what to do I felt happier and a bit relieved as I had worried about making it on the Cape Wrath Trail as it is very challenging and requires carrying multi-day supplies of food.

On the news front I learnt that we now had a new prime minister, Riki Sumak. Liz Truss had lasted all of 44 days which means she will go down in history as the shortest office as prime minister beating the previous record by one day (but then that PM died).

It was raining in the morning, a leg inspection showed it to be no worse, I would attempt to walk, though if the rain continued I was tempted to catch a bus as I could be home in a day. I set off along the forestry track passing warning signs regarding forestry works. A little later there were some caravans by the track presumably to house the workers and then I arrived at a barrier. The man spoke on a walkie-talkie and I was allowed through. The loggers were up above the track but trees had been felled right down to the track and so at times you cannot pass. I came to a second barrier, this one 'manned' by a woman in her sixties who offered me a chocolate éclair sweet! (another first on a walk). We chatted and she explained that she had been there since the previous March giving visions of her car stashed full of chocolate eclairs to offer passing walkers and cyclists. Normally she explained a route would be closed but this is a national trail and there are no possible diversions so she had been brought in to help (her husband was working the machines). I suppose it could be quite interesting meeting different people.

Later the Great Glen Way has been diverted up the hill to bypass a large area which is being developed for hydroelectric power above Loch Lochy. There were information boards explaining the process and the size of the lochs in the Great Glen. I dropped down to Laggan Lochs and had a break, the rain had stopped quite a bit earlier and the weather was mild. There is a large barge there, the 'Eagle Barge Café' but it was closed for the season, the 'story' of my walk, everything closed. Beyond Lagan the route passes through an area of mixed woodland with massive redwoods and ferns.

Meeting a road I walked past the Great Glen water park which is beside Loch Oich. The wooden chalets all looked rather sad and rundown but perhaps that was because the site was closed for the winter. There is an old railway station at Invergarry which is going to be renovated and had a few trains there. I presumed the line went somewhere but the old track has been made into the Great Glen Way so I wasn't very sure of the point of renovating a station to nowhere.

I saw lots of cyclists as this section of the Great Glen Way is much more suited to cycling than walking. One couple had a child's trailer so the dog could ride along. I came across a bare-foot cyclist taking a photo of a rainbow. I was intrigued by his lack of shoes, he just evidently doesn't like wearing them! (he lives in Devon so I suppose it is warmer there). He did confess to having worn shoes a few days earlier to walk up Ben Nevis, he may have been one of the headtorches I had seen ascending. I followed the railway line for four miles, old railway lines were a familiar part of my walk I realised. I had followed one from Monmouth to Lydbrook, Innerleithen to Peebles and one on the Pennine Way from Alston.

In the afternoon I began to struggle, my ankle did not hurt but I found I was weary and the tracks were hard on my feet. I also thought about all the unnecessary things I was carrying; maps for the other route, river shoes for all the crossings I would have taken, gaiters for the snow I might have encountered, warm gloves, an extra jumper and probably more things. Perhaps I would just get to Fort Augustus and then stop.

At Oich Bridge the traffic was queuing to wait for the bridge over the river to close which had opened for leisure boats. The boats have to queue too as there are locks. I was now beside the Caledonian canal which links Loch Ness to Loch Oich. I wanted to camp soon but realised I didn't have any water, there was plenty of water in the canal but I was pretty sure that was not for drinking. I knocked on the door of a former lock keepers' cottage and asked for my bottle to be filled up, hoping they might offer me a cup of tea, they didn't.

I found a wide area of grass by the Caledonian canal and put my tent up and fell asleep. Later I wandered by the canal in the late evening, there was no wind and the golden leaves reflected in the water with a few bats flitting above. I decided I would walk to Fort Augustus in the morning and head home, I was too weary to continue and should probably rest my leg.

It was a very pleasant walk to Fort Augustus, the canal reflected a golden sunrise. I met the lock keeper at Kytra lock, he had driven from Blairgowrie which seemed a long way. Of course all the old lock keepers' houses were sold for lots of money so now the keepers commute in. He would have had a quiet hour or so before any boats appeared.

I arrived in Fort Augustus and went into a café for coffee. I chatted to some tourists from Germany and Alaska. The conversation turned to identity and community, reminding me of the chat with the man in the churchyard all that way away in Kent. The lady from Alaska explained that her husband had dementia and this trip with her daughter and grandchildren (who live in Germany) was for him to revisit the places he knew in Scotland from his mountaineering days. He had also been a famous dog musher in Alaska and so she explained that his community was the world of mountaineers and dog sledding not just where they lived. He was a cheery, jokey man, enjoying his trip even though he evidently couldn't remember each day.

As I left the cafe it began to rain hard, I didn't want to walk any more, I headed off to catch a bus home.

Chapter 17

Fort Augustus to Ullapool-waterfalls and water
16th-22nd March 2023

It was March again, nearly a year since I had been forced to stop my walk, definitely time to finish the final section. It would be good to complete the walk within the year. I had thought about which route to take and as to whether I would return to Fort William and pick up the Cape Wrath trail again to Ullapool. This would mean carrying multi-days supplies of food and I was apprehensive to carry too heavy a pack. Studying the maps with Martha she helped me find a route up the Great Glen towards Inverness and then across west of Inverness to Contin, which is on the Inverness to Ullapool road. From there I could head into the hills and drop down into Ullapool from the east, a route I have often walked. It would give a varied walk of forests, minor roads and then mountains. It also meant I would not have to carry more than a couple of days-worth of food until the last three days. I had also discovered that I rather enjoyed walking through places where there were people rather than just in wild areas.

On a local walk I had met a man out checking the route of the Hebridean Way in preparation for leading groups along it in 2024. He is part of a company who guide clients on various walks including the Cape Wrath trail. Out of interest I looked up how much they charge for such trips, nearly £1,600 for seven nights on just part of the trail! Somewhat out of my price range! However there are people who have the money to pay for guided walks and so it is nice they exist. Thinking about the guides on these walks it occurred to me that I had missed my vocation, imagine being paid to walk!

I wasn't sure though that I would find it easy walking with too many people and would find it cheating to be ferried to a comfortable hotel at the end of each day. There is something satisfying in the continuity of getting up and continuing walking from the same point where you slept out in the land. In some ways my walk was from Ramsgate to Tyndrum as that was completed in one go, the rest felt like 'add ons'. I did though want to complete what I had set out to do and walk all the way back to Ullapool, to have seen the entire route.

It was a wet day as I headed south on the bus to Fort Augustus but I emerged from the bus in warmth and sunshine. I joined the Great Glen Way climbing up into mixed woodland with a big smile on my face, it felt good to be back on the walk. The ground was covered in thick mosses with ferns growing out of cracks in the rocks. The clover-like leaves of wood sorrel pushing up through the moss. Before leaving I had read some disparaging comments online about this section of the Great Glen Way, one man suggesting that the only nice parts of the way were south of Fort Augustus. This section north he described as thick plantations. I disagree, coming from the Isle of Lewis where the only tall trees are in Stornoway castle grounds it is a treat to walk for miles amongst trees. There is a mix too of tall straight firs, silver birch and some alders before entering dense pines. The track was a carpet of soft pine needles and littered with decaying pine cones. Above, bunches of chestnut-coloured cones hung on the high branches against the blue sky. Birds sang, robins, finches, the chattering of tits and the barely audible squeaks of goldcrests. Perhaps if the day had been overcast I may have felt different but to me this section of the Great Glen Way was very beautiful.

The hillside down to Loch Ness is very steep so the road was hidden from view and the track crosses many small but impressive waterfalls. Loch Ness isn't the most scenic of lochs as it is so large with straight wooded sides but its sheer size makes it impressive. It has the largest volume of any loch, though loch Lomond has a bigger surface area. I looked for Nessie but he could have been anywhere. Horizontal clouds drifted above the loch before suddenly thick clouds obscured the view. The loch disappeared allowing Nessie to practise acrobatics unobserved by passing motorists and myself.

Nearing Invermoriston I passed several folk out walking and two dogs, Toto and Sherlock. It's a long descent down to the valley and Invermoriston where there are impressive waterfalls as the river cuts through a gorge. I found a hidden spot in the woods to set up camp and even had the luxury of nearby public toilets!

It rained in the night but was dry the next morning as I climbed up out of the valley back into the woods. Song birds sang and a woodpecker was busy drumming. Wood pigeons continued their plaintive call "my feet hurt Betty", but my feet were fine, thank you. There is a choice of a high route or a low route on the section to Drumnadrochit. I chose the high route with the promise of views. In fact the sign claims to give you 'never before seen views' of the Monadhliath mountains! That seemed a conceited claim, who knows who wandered these hills throughout the centuries. The high route goes above the forestry and does give great views; Ben Nevis was hidden in cloud but the Monadhliath mountains the other side of the loch appeared as a vast plateau splattered with snow.

Clouds hung in the valleys, drifting up like smoke. The path twisted up and down crossing small side valleys. Birds sung and a robin hopped from tree to tree before darting down to snatch a worm almost from under my feet. Joining a forestry track through monotonous plantations it began to rain. I noted immense ant hills and started to hear the song "the ants went marching one by one…." in my head. I had recently seen a kids' TV programme with my grand-daughter, the CGI ants appearing to float as they marched off, it was quite mesmerising.

The plantations ended at old woodland with lichen covered trees and signs of rootling by wild boar. A high road passes scattered houses on rough heathland before a long descent to Drumnadrochit. I had walked through the village in 2013 but since then it has grown considerably. Children were being coached in shinty, I had never seen the game played before. It appears to be a violent form of hockey, everyone wearing face guards and helmets. I shopped in the co op then went for a meal in the only place open. I was hungry, I could have eaten two meals. A couple nearby had big rucksacks and were studying a large. glossy guide book. They donned down jackets and waterproof jackets on leaving, they must have felt the cold to walk in so much, the weather was mild.

The Great Glen Way continues on the road out of Drumnadrochit, the village seemed a bit sad with so few visitors. In the summer it is a busy place. I wondered about camping by the ferry pier but it was too close to the road and the grass not flat so I found a spot further on. I had caught the ferry across the loch to Inverfarigaig here on my 2013 TGO crossing. There were several of us waiting for the ferry to return and once it arrived the ferry man expressed some concern that the weather was deteriorating and asked whether we wanted to still sail. One man did diplomatically suggest that it was up to the ferryman to decide as he would have to return too. We crossed, it didn't seem that rough, the only disconcerting thing was being told how deep the loch is once we were in the middle.

The best view of Urquahart castle must be from the Great Glen Way, it is certainly not very visible from the road. I had a good view of it in the morning from my tent. The next two days I was mostly road walking to get to the west of Inverness. To start with I continued on the Great Glen Way as far as the Abriachin forest centre where there are activities for children and adults; cycle jumps, walks, classrooms, play area and café (which was ofcourse closed). The forest enroute there had a carpet of verdant green moss and a strong sweet smell reminiscent of strawberry jam. Perhaps that is why pine martins like jam, it's the smell of the forest. Signs indicated there were pine martins in the area, I did not see one but then I was not carrying any jam on me.

After the forest centre I left the Great Glen Way, which continues to Inverness, to head north west along roads. I resisted the temptation of 'granny Julia's famous lemon cake' at Abriachin eco-campsite. It would have been a 2km detour and it would probably be closed. Descending to the river Beauly I hadn't realised how high up I had been until the road kept going down and down apparently for miles. There was little traffic, the greatest danger being from cyclists zooming down, it must be an exhilarating ride but not if you crash into a lone back-packer. Wide reaching views over the valley led to snow covered mountains further north, the woods changed to beech trees. Old trees clung precariously to the steep banks by the road their roots exposed, threatening to topple over.

In Kiltarlity I stopped on a bench on the hill to eat lunch. When I got up I read the plaque on the bench; it had been erected by two councillors "for senior citizens to rest their weary legs"! Tough luck to any weary younger folk. I now have a bus pass so I presume count as a senior citizen! Nearby is Beaufort castle and I had hoped to walk through the estate cutting off some road. It is possible to walk in the estate but near the castle is a sign "private, please respect our privacy" so you cannot walk in front of the castle though who is going to be able to look into their living room? It meant I did a big loop to miss out a short section of road.

I crossed the river Beauly at Kilmorack, the area feels violated as it is where the tall pylons from Denny cross. Some pylons have been erected directly in front of the few houses. Nearby is a massive electrical substation and the gravel pit on my map has now consumed Balbair wood and almost meets the river. Planning notification by a small road is for a large electrical storage site. The next day in Contin I learnt that high pylons, taller than any in Britain are going to pass through the area bringing 'green' electricity from off shore to the site near Beauly.

I followed quiet roads north past large houses set in big gardens. There was a dearth of footpaths, the land fenced off. By Rheindown wood the houses were smaller overlooking the valley with their backs to the wood. Some people have cut the verge by the wood and planted shrubs, one house creating a 'fairy' garden with a seat. Others have grown tall hedges or have fences shutting out any view of the woods. Birds sang and a red squirrel ran down the road. A path led through the woods which had old lichen-covered trees and tussocky undergrowth of heather, moss and bilberry bushes.

Later I wanted to avoid Muir of Ord so headed up a path marked on my map. All was fine until I met an area of forestry, it had been felled and the great trunks were being gathered up by a very large grabbing machine. I gave the machine a wide berth as I attempted to find the path. The man stopped and pointed out what he thought was the way and I headed down a rough path to meet a wall of gorse. Beyond was the fence, a deer fence. I couldn't go back through the forestry and the path on my map was by the fence except it was blocked off. I managed to find a way through the gorse to reach the deer fence noticing an electric fence the other side. So I shimmied over the fence, pack, poles and all. Well no, you shouldn't really climb over deer fences as it damages them but I found a section with wooden railing the other side. Standing on the wooden rail I threw my pack over. I was committed then to joining my pack but climbing over packless was easy and I avoided standing on the electric fence. Meeting an old track beside the wood I followed it to arrive at more fences. I eventually reached a road by crossing a sheep field, the sheep looking surprised with sticking up 'rabbit's' ears. Reaching the road via a new-build site I thought perhaps the route through Muir of Ord would have been easier.

To reach Contin I needed to cross the river Conon and the only bridge for miles is at Marybank which meant two miles walking along the main Inverness to Ullapool road. Thankfully a nice motorist stopped and drove me there in a matter of minutes. Stocking up for the next few days in the village shop I bought their stock of Danish pastries, individually plastic wrapped but baked in nearby Dingwall and surprisingly E less. I bought one to eat outside with a take-away coffee, I felt empty. Contin is a bit run-down, route 500 passes through but there isn't much to stop for.

There are no cafes, public toilets or pubs and the school is shut. There were no toilets either at the nearby cycle trail parking, not until April. Plenty of trees and bushes in the meantime.

I set off along the cycle track to Garve greeting two cheery middle-aged cyclists photographing the two large chain-saw bear sculptures. I am not sure what happened to 'baby' bear. I overtook the cyclists later pushing their bicycles as the track becomes very steep and rocky enroute to Rogie. Abandoning my pack I detoured down to the falls which are very impressive with spray drifting off the water. There is a rather vertiginous suspension bridge crossing the river.

I camped in the woods before Garve, it rained again in the night and in the morning water droplets sparkled off the birch trees. I like Garve, there isn't much there, just a train station with infrequent trains and a small school. The hotel closed in lockdown and never reopened and there is no longer a shop and a couple of years ago the post office only opened a couple of hours a week. But I like the woods all around and the happy drivers who waved. There is another impressive waterfall and old stone bridge at Little Garve where I crossed the main road to head north through plantations.

The forestry was dull and the valley there is bleak, miles of plantations many of them being felled. I came to an area with log stacks and notices warning 'danger of death' to not climb on them. They have graphic drawings of stick men being crushed by a log. It started to rain and those ants began marching… Sooner than expected I escaped the forest to walk half a mile along the main road to Strath Rannoch. Faded tourism signs indicate Inchbae Lodge Hotel and I began to think of coffee and food. A couple of cars were parked outside but a closed sign flashed in the window.

Perhaps I was early? I looked at the opening times, every day from mid-day except Tuesdays when they are closed, ofcourse it was Tuesday!

Walking up Strath Rannoch the sun came out and it became quite warm. The land opened out into wide bare valleys with snow covered mountains beyond. I walked over to Strath Vaich where young trees have been planted and there is a large loch. Half way along is an abandoned house and barn where I sheltered once from the rain. There was lots of flat grass to put up my tent and enjoy the sunny evening.

I woke at 5am, it was raining and I could hear the wind but the tent wasn't moving. Then with a great whoosh the wind and a 'power shower' hit my tent. I sat up quickly, spray was getting through and the tent was hitting me, time to get out! Rapidly I put on waterproofs, packed up and took down the tent, beating a hasty retreat to the old house. It still has an intact roof and one room has a wooden floor. I put my mat and sleeping bag down to get some more rest but didn't sleep as it was also very draughty, there being no doors or windows. It wasn't long before it got light so I packed up and attempted unsuccessfully to light the stove, it was too windy.

It was sunny as I left but not for long, soon the rain started but atleast the strong winds were behind me. My plan was to walk through to the next glen and then over the mountains to drop down to a bothy at Corriemore. However the wind was gusting atleast 40mph in the valley, buffeting me around it wasn't sensible to go any higher. It was trying to sleet as well, high up it must have been snowing. I decided to walk out to the road through the Alladale estate and then back up another valley to skirt round the mountains. It would be much further, I wasn't sure how far as I would fall off my map but hopefully I could get to a different bothy that night and so be somewhere dry.

The wind was so strong that when I reached the bridge at Deanich lodge I crossed on hands and knees as it was impossible to stay upright with the side wind! It was an interesting view of the bridge and I took note of any splinters as I didn't want my waterproof trousers to get more torn. Once amongst the trees there was instant shelter from the worst of the wind. Some way down is a badger hide where I dreamt of getting indoors and making a cup of tea. It was locked, I made do with sheltering in the doorway for a quick break. Later the estate man said it had been locked since lockdown to stop misuse. A man had been staying there for four days, it is sad that one person's selfish actions ruins it for all.

There is a spectacular river by the driveway from Alladale lodge but I was wet and tired. I half hoped that the people working on a wooden building by the entrance would invite me for a tea break but perhaps they had already had theirs. I had had nothing hot all day. I heard a vehicle and flagged it down, the kind estate worker took me to the road junction at the end of the valley. I was one mile from Croik church, perhaps that would be unlocked? It was locked, I sheltered behind the church. Atleast I was more fortunate than the eighty people in May 1845 who lived in the churchyard having been cleared from their homes in Glen Calvie to the south. Some of them scratched a record of this on the window panes.

A gate nearby leads back into the hills, a sign informs that it is thirty miles to Ullapool. In 2008 we walked this way on the start of our first back-packing trip. I have a photo of my three children looking slightly daunted at the prospect by the sign. I pulled my hood down firmer, I would now be walking straight into the wind and rain. I put my head down and set off. The start of the valley is bleak with too many sheep and deer on it, I wouldn't be missing much scenery.

Higher up I entered trees and the rain eased off but the path became a river with large pools to by-pass. My waterproof gloves and trousers were soaked through, I hoped they would work like a wetsuit and still keep me warm. In fact a wet suit would have been a good idea. Reaching a deep ford I removed my boots to cross, my feet were still reasonably dry. My gloves were too wet to get back on so I thought it would be alright for the last couple of miles as the rain had stopped.

All along the track I had come across dead, or possibly comatose frogs and even a couple of lizards. I wondered whether it was because of the cold that day and the rain or if perhaps they die having mated and spawned. Frog spawn sat in some of the deeper puddles, the potential young will never get to grow as the water will dry up. However it will make good meals for birds and small mammals, the way of nature.

The weather threw one final blast at me – hailstones and a bitter headwind. I put my head down and increased my pace trying to ignore my completely numb hands. Then the sun burst out and by the time the bothy came into view I was warm and the wind had dried my clothes.

Schoolhouse bothy as the name implies was an old school built to serve the few scattered houses in the valley. It is constructed of corrugated iron and has three rooms, one is insulated with a double glazed window so quite cosy. I was there in January when heavy snow and good weather coincided with my birthday. With relief I went in and made a cup of tea, my first hot drink all day. Going to the bothy 'library' I found the book I had begun reading in January and settled down, I was staying put for the night.

I woke to sun and only a gentle breeze, my last day of my long walk to Ullapool. I have walked this way many times before, it is twenty miles mostly downhill. The only worry I had was the ford a mile from the bothy, would the river be too high to safely cross? It was deeper than I had ever seen it so I removed my trousers as well as my boots to cross but the water only came just above my knees.

After a couple of hours I reached Knockdamph bothy which is an old shepherd's house high up above the loch. Sometimes it is a very cold, bleak spot but in the sunshine it looked welcoming. At the end of the loch I could see the tiny hut where I spent the night before my sixtieth birthday in January. It is a garden shed put there by the Rhidorroch estate but walkers are welcome to use it. There was deep snow around and the hut is well ventilated with holes in places, partly because the cows rub against the walls. There are though two windows which look straight down the loch and I woke to look out on a semi-frozen world. I had been warm but everything was frozen including my boots! I had to defrost the laces to put them on but it was a memorable birthday, walking out in deep snow and sunshine.

The sun was shining again but now it was warm and I kept removing layers as I dropped down into the valley. I detoured to visit an amazing waterfall which though only a little way from the track I had never seen. There is a deep narrow gorge and the water cascades down into it with a roar and billowing clouds of vapour. It was more spectacular than all the tourist falls and better for being remote.

My final detour was to reach Ullapool via Ullapool hill rather than the bleak road beside the quarry which I have always taken. The hill was tricky to access as the farmer feeds the cows in the gateway resulting in deep mud. I shooed the cows away as I needed to stand on the tussocks they were using to save disappearing down into the mud. I had pushed my pole down and saw it sink under several feet! Once on the hill the views were lovely and I looked down on Ullapool and the ferry terminal, my goal.

As I descended I thought about my long walk and all I had seen, I was a long way from Kent. I was pleased I had completed the walk. I had enjoyed my walk, now it was time to go home. I walked through Ullapool to the shore to wait for the ferry which would take me back to the Isle of Lewis.

Appendix

Named walks	distance	location
North Downs Way	153 miles	Dover, Kent to Farnham, Surrey
Greensand Way	108 miles	Hamstreet, Kent to Hazlemere, Surrey
Lea Valley way	50 miles	Leagrave,Beds to Limehouse Basin, London
Hertfordshire Way	194 miles	circular walk
Icknield Way	170 miles	Knettishall Heath, Norfolk to Ivinghoe Beacon, Bucks
The Ridgeway	87 miles	Ivinghoe Beacon, Bucks to Overton Hill, Wiltshire
Oxfordshire Way	68 miles	Henley-on-Thames, Bucks to Bourton-on-the-water, Gloucestershire
Oxford Greenbelt Way	50 miles	circular walk around Oxford

Wychwood Way	36 miles	circular walk in heart of ancient Wychwood forest, Oxfordshire
Winchcombe Way	13.5 miles	Bourton-on-the-water to Winchcombe, Gloucestershire
Gloucestershire Way	100 miles	Chepstow, South Wales to Tewkesbury, Gloucestershire
Offa's Dyke Path	177 miles	Sedbury, South Wales to Prestatyn, North Wales
Wats Dyke Path	61 miles	Llanymynech, Shropshire to Holywell, Flintshire
North Cheshire Way	71 miles	Hooton, Wirral to Disley, Cheshire
Pennine Way	268 miles	Edale, Derbyshire to Kirk Yetholm, Borders
St Cuthbert's Way	116 miles	Lindisfarne, Northumbria to Melrose, Borders
Scottish National Trail	537 miles	Kirk Yetholm, Borders to Cape Wrath, Sutherland

Southern Upland Way	214 miles	Cockburnspath, Borders to Portpartrick, Dumfries & Galloway
John Muir Way	134 miles	Dunbar, East Lothian to Helensburgh, Argyll & Bute
West Highland Way	96 miles	Milngavie, Glasgow to Fort William, Lochaber
Cape Wrath Trail	200 miles	Fort William, Lochaber to Cape Wrath, Sutherland
Great Glen Way	79 miles	Fort William, Lochaber to Inverness, Highlands

TGO The Great Outdoors Challenge annual two week challenge to walk unsupported from west to east across Scotland

Bibliography

Roald Dahl	Big Friendly Giant
John Hillaby	Journey through Britain
Richard Mabey	Home Country
Robert Macfarlane	The Old Ways
Bill Bryson	A Walk in the Woods
Stephen Moss	The Accidental countryside
Cicerone Guide	Offa's Dyke Path
Rachel Joyce	The unlikely pilgrimage of Harold Fry
Cicerone Guide	The Pennine Way
Emily Bronte	Wuthering Heights
Hannah Hauxwell	Hannah, the complete story
Hamish Brown	Three Men on the Way Way
Robert Loius Stevenson	Kidnapped

Appendix 2

Kit list

Paramo waterproof and waterproof trousers

Scarpa walking boots

Walking trousers

Merino wool vest (always worn)

Lightweight merino wool baselayer (worn in south and at end)

Heavier merino wool baselayer (worn in north)

Synthetic long-sleeved top (always worn)

Wool and silk jumper (kept for night time)

Down jacket (kept for camping)

Woollen gloves (barely worn)

Pair of thermal gloves

Pair of waterproof gloves

Woollen hat

Light weight fabric scarf

Tube

2 pairs woollen walking socks (only wore one pair whole time)

Trainers, leggings, t-shirt (for parkruns, sent home on Pennine way)

Lux outer tent and winter inner

Rab down sleeping bag

Rab silk sleeping bag liner

Foam sleeping mat

Gas stove & 2 gas cylinders

2 ancient aluminium pots

Plastic spoon

Knife

Small teatowel

Matches

Small travel towel (sent home)

Toothbrush & toothpaste

Comb

Diary

Pens

Notebook with planned route, addresses etc..

Sections of maps

Pennine way guide (only for that section)

Camera & spare batteries

Headtorch & spare batteries

Phone & charger

First aid kit; plasters, compeed, paracetamol, nurofen, scissors, nail clippers, support bandage

Needle & cotton

Milton Keynes UK
Ingram Content Group UK Ltd.
UKHW021045210224
438109UK00008B/125